GOODBYE WORLD

BY C. LESLIE MILLER

G/L REGAL BOOKS

A Division of G/L Publications
Glendale, California, U.S.A.

Printed in U.S.A.

Published by
Regal Books Division, G/L Publications
Glendale, California 91209, U.S.A.

Library of Congress Catalog Card No. 72-85642
ISBN 0-8307-0192-3

Contents

Foreword

Because of the fast, convulsive events that have occurred in our own century—especially since mankind, devoted to anemic theories of world peace, was suddenly engulfed in the holocaust of the First World War; because of the enormously destructive powers that man has in the last few years stored up in nuclear weapons; and because of this spirit of lawlessness and savagery that is so mysteriously entering into the souls of so many—it is easily understandable why men everywhere are so earnestly asking questions as to what the future may hold for the human race.

Indeed many professors in our universities are offering courses exploring the possibilities of the future in economics, the biological sciences, the intentions of China and Russia, world population, ecology, one world government, even the future of religion. Around these subjects a veritable library of books has been produced, and even a scholarly periodical is being published with the significant title, *The Futurist*. Indeed one may not hesitate in stating that the future is today being more intently scrutinized than at any time since the fall of Rome.

In the midst of this feverish activity in attempting to foreknow what is before us, one group alone has a divine guide for such pursuits, an inspired volume of far-reaching prophecies, and that group is made up of Christian believers who are taught with authority by the inspired pages of Holy Scripture which reveal to us "things to come." Through the ages a rich literature has been created by biblical students who have interpreted for the Church the great themes of biblical prediction, especially since the beginning of the eighteenth century.

In *Goodbye World,* the author has written a very helpful handbook of the study of many of the major prophecies of the Bible that relate to events that are yet to take place. And I would underscore the word *helpful.*

What most impressed me as I carefully read through the manuscript was the vivid way in which he describes the darker phenomena that will develop at the end of this age. He writes as though he were actually present as these events take place. For many, such terms as Antichrist, lawlessness, Armageddon and worldwide unbelief will become terms of greater significance. And beyond the tragedies and sorrows that will accumulate as this age comes to its end will be the coming in power of the Lord of Glory, the hope of the resurrection, a new earth, an age of righteousness, of the rule of the King of kings and an eternity with Him into whose image we who are His will be transformed. What a glorious future!

Wilbur M. Smith, D.D., Litt.D.
Professor Emeritus,
Trinity Evangelical Divinity School
Member of the Revision Committee,
Schofield Reference Bible

Author's Introduction

It happened in a lovely dining room overlooking the blue Pacific. There were three of us and the remark was made, "What is needed is a simple, interesting and easily understood book on biblical prophecy."

We had been talking about the Jesus People and other new converts who have had little or no biblical or evangelical background or teaching but through their insatiable appetite for the Word of God were discovering the exciting realm of biblical prophecy. Many excellent books on this subject are available but most of them have been written for the mature Christian with years of Bible reading experience.

And then came the challenge. "Why don't *you* write the kind of book these young people will read and can understand?"

Within a few minutes a book outline and chapter titles were scribbled on a paper napkin. And thus was conceived, *"GOODBYE WORLD."*

The writer makes no apology for the use of the King James Version of the Bible. It may not be the best, but it remains the most widely read version.

No attempt has been made to conceal my conservative dispensational position nor my moderately literalistic interpretation of Revelation.

Also, it will soon become evident to the reader that the author believes the Church and the Holy Spirit will "be taken out of the way [before], that man of sin . . . the son of perdition be revealed."*

The writer holds to the position that the hope of the church is not the coming of the Great Tribulation but the imminent appearing of our Lord and Saviour Jesus Christ.

The wise counsel and encouragement of several associates and my wife Pearl have played a major part in bringing this book to its final stage of production.

For any good that may be accomplished through its distribution, all the glory must go to God.

For any mistaken interpretation or error, we shall apologize when we no longer "know in part" nor "see through a glass darkly" but shall know as we are known.

C. Leslie Miller

* II Thessalonians 2:3-8

CHAPTER 1

The Importance of Prophecy

The prophecy gap started with the disciples of Jesus. They had some knowledge of their Scriptures but it is evident that their understanding of prophecy was woefully limited. Throughout His teaching ministry the Lord Jesus was constantly referring to and quoting the Old Testament prophets. Like many Christians today, the disciples either were not interested or did not consider such knowledge of sufficient importance to call for the investment of time and study.

Consequently, the atoning death and resurrection of Christ caught them completely by surprise. Possibly, Peter would not have denied His Lord had he, through an understanding of the prophecies, fully comprehended the mission of the suffering Messiah. Another interesting question: Would Judas have betrayed Jesus had he been familiar with and understood David's prophecies concerning that betrayal?[1]

The two disciples who met Jesus, on the day of His resurrection as they approached Emmaus, were astonished as "he expounded unto them in all the scriptures the things concerning himself." In fact, He sharply rebuked them for their ignorance of prophecy, "O fools, and slow of heart to believe all that the prophets have spoken."[2]

All this brings us to the conclusion that study and an understanding of biblical prophecy is of inestimable importance to every Christian. All Bible study is important and results in blessing and spiritual growth, but only of prophetic study does the Bible declare, "Blessed is he that readeth, and they that hear the words of this prophecy, and keep those things which are written therein: for the time is at hand."[3]

Extensive Coverage

The importance of biblical prophecy is indicated by the extensive coverage given to it in the Word of God. The story of man's destiny begins with prophecy and its golden thread becomes a broad band as it progresses through divine revelation. Major books and major portions of other books of the Bible are devoted to it. It is likely that when we no longer "see in part and understand in part," we shall discover that every book of the Bible was to some extent prophetic. History, the Law, the poetical portions, the Gospels, the Acts of the Holy Spirit, the Epistles—all point to the coming Redeemer . . . the Coming King of kings and Lord of lords and are therefore prophetic.

Evidence of Inspiration

The trumpets are blaring, the battle flags are unfurled and combat lines are drawn as theological forces clash over conflicting viewpoints of the inerrancy and inspiration of the Bible. While the conflict rages, the layman who loves the Bible and believes it to be the Word of God, which came to us as "holy men of God spake . . . moved by the Holy Ghost,"[4] continues to find his faith fortified as he discovers in the Scriptures the vast hosts of prophecies which have been fulfilled. Choice passages include the detailed crucifixion story of Psalm 22; Isaiah's paradoxical account of the execution and burial of the suffering Messiah in his fifty-third chapter; Isaiah's naming of Cyrus before he was born,[5] the many prophecies concerning the birth and nativity of Jesus. These and multitudes of others all say to the student of the Bible, "All scripture is given by inspiration of God."[6]

Christ's Emphasis

When the twelve-year-old son of Mary was found in the Temple, He was "sitting in the midst of the doctors, both hearing them, and asking them questions. And all that heard him were astonished at his understanding and answers."[7] What were they discussing? The laws of Moses? It's not likely. Those were fixed and already overdeveloped by the Talmud until there was little rhyme or reason for discussion. But prophecy? That was different. Every faithful son of Abraham through of little else in those dark days of oppression. The subsequent teaching of Jesus would indicate He may have been discussing with the doctors all that Moses and the prophets wrote concerning Himself.

An interesting feature of the preaching ministry of Billy Graham is his repetitious statement, "The Bible says. . . ." This did not originate with Billy, but with Jesus. Again and again, almost with monotonous repetition, there it is on page after page of the Gospels: "It is written . . . that the Scriptures might be fulfilled." And whenever Jesus used these words He was referring to prophecy! He believed in it. He knew it and used it in His teaching. Frequently Jesus rebuked His disciples for their ignorance of prophecy.

Not only did the Lord Jesus Christ quote prophecy and fulfill it, He also created it. A surprising portion of His teaching deals with future events. More about this later.

Historical Problems

Church history is filled with examples of tragic conflicts and lasting divisions in the Christian community which can be traced to an ignorance or misunderstanding of prophetic Scriptures. Wars have been fought, generations have perished without the Gospel, cults have arisen, continents have remained unevangelized—all, to some extent at least, because the Christian church has ignored the vital importance of understanding and teaching biblical prophecy.

Strange, is it not, that many strongly evangelical churches know little or nothing about this important part of "all scripture"? Some of the most zealous defenders of the faith who are excellent Bible teachers seldom open the prophetic Scriptures to their congregations. The result? An atmosphere of mystery and even suspicion is evident in the attitude of most Christians with regard to prophetic study.

If we truly believe that "all scripture is given by inspiration of God, and is profitable . . ." then why detour around the prophetic Scriptures? And that question suggests another one. In what way are the prophetic Scriptures profitable?

A Purifying Agent

The return of the Lord Jesus Christ is the focus of prophetic matter. In the New Testament it is called "that blessed hope" and "this hope."[8] In writing to Titus, Paul emphasizes the blessing aspect of the prophecy which promises the return of our blessed Lord. The apostle John called attention to its purifying power. Whenever a local congregation places a proper emphasis upon the imminent return of Christ in its teaching and preaching, it will develop a spiritual and moral purity that will delight the heart of God and add a new dimension of effectiveness to its witness.

It is important to notice that John did not say that a *belief* in that blessed hope would have a purifying effect. Rather, the *possession* of it purifies the believer. "Every man that *hath* this hope." No Christian will deliberately lie or steal or commit fornication while "that blessed hope" is filling his soul. *Before* we willfully sin we delete from our conscious mind the hope of the Lord's return. Only when first we stop "lifting up our heads" to our approaching redemption do we look down and see the glittering fool's gold of this world's pleasures. Demas, Paul's young and promising assistant, had to fall out of love with Jesus Christ before falling in love with this present world.

An Activating Catalyst

The apostle Peter referred to the second appearing of Christ as "a lively [living] hope."[9] The prophetic truth of Christ's return, when assimilated as part of the spiritual fiber, galvanizes a Christian and a church to evangelical action. It was Christ's promise, "I will come again," that added urgency to His command, "Go ye into all the world." An assembly of believers that emphasizes the Lord's return is inevitably a missionary church. Knowing that He may come today, and really believing it, will get any Christian off his seat and onto his feet for God and for souls. Realizing that "the night is far spent and the day is at hand" will keep us from going back to bed. As we see the approaching sunrise of Christ's appearing we realize that it's time to go to work.

Pastor Shireman was an old man and I was in my teens. I don't remember any doctrinal sermons he preached, but I do remember two things about his ministry. Most of what I know about biblical prophecy I learned under his guidance and inspiration. Second, over his desk was a placard with two words printed in bright hues. He was a tireless man, always active visiting, teaching, praying and sometimes weeping (over my waywardness). Many times I saw him sink into his desk chair almost too weary to hold up his head. And then he would raise his eyes to that placard. Suddenly something happened. He squared his aged shoulders; a new light came into his eyes and he was ready to get going again. The two words: TODAY? PERHAPS!

Footnotes

1. Psalm 41:9; 69:25
2. Luke 24:25-27
3. Revelation 1:3
4. II Peter 1:21
5. Isaiah 44:28; 45:1
6. II Timothy 3:16
7. Luke 2:46,47
8. Titus 2:13; I John 3:3
9. I Peter 1:3

CHAPTER 2

What Do They Mean?

A school teacher complained that her students were suffering from "Dictionary Deficiency." When an explanation was demanded she replied, "Their vocabulary is too limited, they make no effort to learn new words and they do not know the definitions of most of the words they do use." The same statement could be made of many students and teachers of prophecy.

The study of prophecy has produced its own vocabulary and not all of it is biblical in origin. The misunderstanding or misuse of words and terms comprising this vocabulary has eventuated in endless confusion and occasionally in gross error.

Before beginning a study of prophetic Scripture a serious student should determine correct definitions of the terms commonly used in the Bible, and by those who teach and write on prophecy. Only then will the pieces of the prophetic jigsaw puzzle fall into their proper positions and reveal the exciting and beautiful landscape of the ages painted by the eternal brush of God.

Following are some of the prophetic terms most commonly used.

ESCHATOLOGY—(from the Greek *eschator,* the last, furthest)

This word is frequently used in prophetic books and lectures. It means the doctrine of the last or final things, the eventual invasion of the divine will into the affairs of man. It deals with questions related to the end times—the resurrection, the second coming of Christ, the judgments and the final destiny of the world and of man.

THE RAPTURE

This term is not biblical but is frequently used in reference to the Second Appearing of Christ in the air to receive His body, the Church, unto Himself. The biblical term for this event is "the second appearing."[1]

Paul supplied us with a detailed description of this event when he assured the believers of the Thessalonian church that those who had died in Christ had not perished.[2]

In Paul's first letter to the Corinthians he emphasized the resurrection aspect of the "second appearing."[3] Actually this term originated with Paul and it is to this "glorious appearing" that he most frequently referred in his Epistles. This was his "blessed hope" that he shared with his children in the faith.[4]

The Second Appearing is sometimes described as "the translation" of the Church.

THE SECOND COMING OF CHRIST

This term is frequently but mistakenly applied to the "Second Appearing" of Christ for the Church. When the Lord Jesus Christ descends from Heaven to receive His own unto Himself He will appear, not *on* the earth, but in the air. The Church will be caught *up* to meet the Lord.

At the Second Coming of Christ, He will come *on* the earth. "His feet shall stand in that day upon the mount of Olives."[5] Paul refers to this coming as the "revealing" of Christ.[6]

The apostle John gives considerable coverage to the second coming of Christ in his Revelation.[7]

THE DAY OF THE LORD

In describing the day of the Lord, Peter wrote that the heavens and the earth shall pass away and all things shall be dissolved, and there will be new heavens and a new earth.[8]

John referred to the same cataclysmic change, providing much detail of the new heaven and the new earth.[9]

ANTICHRIST

This sinister character caught Daniel's attention and that great prophet used both historical symbolism and prophetic description to portray him.[10]

Paul called him "that man of sin . . . the son of perdition . . . that wicked."[11]

John describes him as "the beast that ascended out of the bottomless pit."[12] His power, his ambitions, his miracles and his final doom will be studied in a later chapter.

THE FALSE PROPHET

This promotion agent of the Antichrist is pictured by John as "another beast coming up out of the earth."[13] He will serve as the high priest of the Antichrist and will enforce blasphemous worship of him.

THE TWO WITNESSES

These two men of mystery appear once in John's prophecy[14] and once in Old Testament prophecy.[15] They will witness for God during the last half of the Tribulation period and will exercise miraculous powers of judgment similar to those performed by Moses in Egypt. They will be indestructible until the completion of their ministry. Then they will be murdered by the Antichrist, but after three and a half days they will be raised to life and will ascend to heaven.

THE 144,000

John clearly reveals in the Revelation that these men will be Israelites, not Gentiles or Christians, who during the Tribulation will be placed under a protective divine seal.[16] Revelation emphasizes that the sealed Israelites are Jews, are unmarried, and are morally perfect before God.

THE GREAT TRIBULATION

There are various interpretations of this prophetic period. All agree that it will be a seven-year period during which the Antichrist will establish his Satanic kingdom. The relation of the Church to this Tribulation period is the point of disagreement. The "*PRE*tribulationists" believe that the Second Appearing of Christ for the Church will occur before the tribulation begins. The "*MID*tribulationists" believe that the Church will remain on the earth to experience the first half of the Great Tribulation. Then there are those who believe the Church will go through the entire seven years of tribulation.

The Great Tribulation will be a time of unprecedented judgment and horror as the wrath of God is poured out upon the kingdom of the Antichrist.[17]

SIGNS OF THE TIMES

These are events predicted by prophetic Scripture as indications of the near approach of the end times. Most of them refer to the Second Coming of Christ and none of them refers directly to the Second Appearing of Christ for the Church. Many of these "signs" were given by Jesus in His great Olivet Discourse.[18]

MILLENNIUM

This is not a biblical term but comes from a Latin word meaning a thousand + year (mille + annus). As used in reference to prophecy it refers to the reign of Christ on this earth following His Second

Coming at the close of the Great Tribulation. Old Testament prophets frequently referred to this Messianic reign of Christ, but its specific duration is given only in Revelation.[19] In glowing terms the prophets described earth's release from the curse and the universal kingdom of peace and righteousness. The apostle Paul also made reference to the release of the creation from its bondage.[20]

BATTLE OF ARMAGEDDON

In Revelation, John gives the geographical location of the final great conflict between the forces of the Antichrist and the Lord Jesus Christ.[21] Armageddon comes from the word *Har-Magedon,* "Mountain of Megiddo." Megiddo was one of history's greatest battlefields.[22] It is to this final battle that God summons the beasts and birds of prey to eat the flesh of great men.[23]

In defining these prophetic terms it is important to remember that the central figure and theme of biblical prophecy is the Lord Jesus Christ. The greatest of all prophetic books, the Revelation, is not the revelation of the Antichrist or the False Prophet, or Armageddon or the Millennium but of Christ Himself.

While it is important to understand the vocabulary of prophecy, it is vastly more important to know Christ, for only in that knowledge is there life eternal.

If your interest in biblical prophecy is only to have a crystal-ball experience to satisfy your innate curiosity about the future, you will never understand prophecy and you will never know Christ.

But if you approach this study with an insatiable desire to know the Jesus of history and the Jesus of glory—Saviour and King of kings—then this study will be one of the richest and most rewarding experiences of your life.

Footnotes

1. Colossians 3:4; Hebrews 9:26-28
2. I Thessalonians 4:14-18
3. I Corinthians 15:51-57
4. Titus 2:13
5. Zechariah 14:4
6. II Thessalonians 1:7-10
7. Revelation 14:14-20; 19:11-21
8. II Peter 3:10-13
9. Revelation 20:11–21:27
10. Daniel 7:19-27; 8:9-12,23-25; 11:31-45
11. II Thessalonians 2:3,8
12. Revelation 11:7; 13:1-8; 17:8-14
13. Revelation 13:11-17
14. Revelation 11:3-13
15. Zechariah 4:11-14
16. Revelation 7:4-8; 14:1-5
17. Revelation 6; 8-11; 15
18. Matthew 24; Mark 13; Luke 21
19. Revelation 20:3,4
20. Romans 8:19-23
21. Revelation 16:16
22. II Kings 9:27; 23:29; II Chronicles 35:22
23. Revelation 19:17-21

CHAPTER 3

Jesus, the Prophet

Jesus: Teacher, Master, Son of God, Healer, Saviour, Risen Lord, Advocate and Coming King. He was all these and one more. He was a Prophet—the greatest of all prophets. Strange, is it not, that one rarely hears of this title being credited to Him?

With understandable pride the disciples called the attention of Jesus to the buildings of the Temple complex, the massive stones and priceless materials used in its construction. Forty-three years it had been in the building process! Then came the Saviour's stunning reaction. "There shall not be left here one stone upon another, that shall not be thrown down."[1]

The shock of that prophetic statement was so great that the disciples were speechless as the group wended its way down the narrow, winding road, across the Kidron Brook, past Gethsemane and up the slope to the Mount of Olives. Then in a veritable torrent the questions came. "Tell us, when shall these things be? What shall be the sign of thy coming, and of the end of the world?"[2]

The questions launched Jesus into the most astonishing series of prophecies to be found in the Bible.

Jesus foretold the destruction of the Temple and the city of Jerusalem.[3] This was fulfilled about forty years later when Titus with his Roman legions broke through the improvised but valiantly defended fortifications, slaughtered the Jews and leveled the city and the Temple.

Jesus, the Prophet, foretold the coming of many false leaders, cultists and apostates.[4] This began to be fulfilled in the later years of the apostle John, and continues to be fulfilled today. This prophecy will culminate in the appearance of the Antichrist and his demand to be worshiped as god.

Jesus prophesied the coming international unrest with its unending series of wars and threats of war.[5] The fulfillment of this prophecy of our Lord has bathed the world in blood and will continue to do so until the Prince of Peace establishes His kingdom of peace and justice. In the meantime, no human agency or effort will stem this evil tide of conflict.

In this great discourse the disciples were warned to expect unprecedented and continuous persecution.[6] Within a few years after Jesus gave this warning, Saul of Tarsus hounded the Christians to death.

Soon the Roman Empire made the persecution of Christians a national sport. Even today, only God knows all the grim stories of suffering and death endured by believers behind the Iron and the Bamboo Curtains.

Some of Jesus' prophecies are just now being fulfilled. He foretold the evangelization of the world,[7] and the release of Jerusalem from Gentile governments.[8] Many missionary organizations, using the most modern media and equipment, are bringing the Gospel to all nations. The release of Jerusalem came during the six-day war. This was one of the most dramatic fulfillments of prophecy ever witnessed. This alone should cause us believers to lift up our heads and realize that our redemption draws nigh.

Some of the horrors of the Great Tribulation judgments are referred to in the prophecies of Jesus.[9] The alarming increase in the number of cardiac victims may be a partial fulfillment of Luke's version of the Olivet Discourse, "Men's hearts failing them for fear."[10]

Of course, Jesus foretold His Second Coming "in the clouds of heaven with power and great glory."[11] And while this great prophetic discourse does not deal directly with our Blessed Hope, it does speak to us in words of solemn exhortation: "Be watching" . . . "Be ready."

Christ's prophecies were not confined to the Olivet Discourse. Jesus foretold the coming of the Holy Spirit upon the disciples.[12] He frequently foretold His death and resurrection. When the disciples were saddened by His announcement that He would be leaving them shortly, He gave them a prophetic promise of His return to comfort them.[13]

The list of Christ's prophecies is long. Jesus foretold Peter's denial[14] and His betrayal by Judas.[15] He prophesied that the anointing of His head by Mary would become an event known worldwide.[16]

But there is yet another prophecy by Jesus that deserves our careful attention, especially in these days of widespread spiritual renewals. Jesus prophesied, "He that believeth on me, the works that I do shall he do also; and greater works than these shall he do; because I go unto my Father."[17] This prophecy is followed by Christ's promise, "Whatsoever ye shall ask in my name, that will I do, that the Father may be glorified in the Son. If ye shall ask any thing in my name, I will do it."[18]

Many Christians believe that the "greater works" refer to the greater success of evangelism experienced by the Church. There are others who believe that the "greater works" refer to the operation of the gifts of the Holy Spirit, including miracles and healings. Still others believe that both greater evangelism and greater supernatural manifestations of God's power were in the mind of Christ when He made that prophecy.

There can be no doubt that whenever Jesus spoke of His "works" He was referring not only to His ministry of teaching and preaching, but also to his miracles of healing, casting out demons, multiplying the loaves and fish, turning water into wine and other supernatural demonstrations of divine power. Twelve times in John's Gospel alone Jesus spoke of His miracles as His "works." So when Jesus prophesied that "greater works" would be done by him "that believeth on me," He not only had evangelism in mind but also actual supernatural works.

During the days of the apostles, "greater" works were done in the name of Jesus. In one day thousands were swept into God's Kingdom. Even Peter's shadow brought healing to the sick. These never happened in the ministry of Jesus. But for centuries the fulfillment of this prophecy had been either terminated or suspended. Within the last century men, women and certain denominations have claimed a renewal of the ministry of miracles. While this, as with all other Christian ministries, has been imitated by Satan and abused or misused by some people, the fact remains that both physical, emotional and spiritual benefits have been and are being experienced by many thousands of souls. But even more important is the moving of the Spirit in regenerating power in the lives of great numbers of people.

Within the last several years, in far off Indonesia, the impossible has happened. An incredible, dynamic spiritual awakening has come to the Moslem population! Missionaries have labored among the Moslems for as long as twenty years without seeing one soul accept Christ. Now in Indonesia not hundreds, but thousands and tens of thousands of Moslems have turned to Christ, and Heaven has come down to that pagan land.

These converts, with no biblical or Christian background whatever, have been naive enough to take the promises and prophecies of Jesus literally. They have believed that Jesus Christ is the same yesterday, forever and *today*. Expecting the omnipotent God to be omnipotent, these spiritual infants have taken His Word at face value and have asked for miracles. And they have happened! Incredible, unbelievable but well documented miracles have occurred and are still occurring!

Here is a contemporary fulfillment of a prophecy made by Jesus more than nineteen hundred years ago.

Yes, Jesus was the master Prophet. We can trust His promises because time has proven that His prophecies are reliable.

Footnotes

1. Matthew 24:2
2. Matthew 24:3
3. Luke 21:20-24
4. Matthew 24:5,23-26
5. Matthew 24:6,7
6. Matthew 24:8-10; Mark 13:9-13
7. Matthew 24:14
8. Luke 21:24
9. Matthew 24:29; Luke 21:11,25,26
10. Luke 21:26
11. Matthew 24:30,31
12. John 14:16,26; 15:26
13. John 14:1-4
14. Matthew 26:34
15. Matthew 26:21-25
16. Matthew 26:6-13
17. John 14:12
18. John 14:13,14

CHAPTER 4

They Also Were Prophets

Paul's reputation for evangelism is unparalleled in Christian history. So intensive and extensive was his ministry that Luke was able to write, ". . . all they which dwelt in Asia heard the word of the Lord Jesus."[1] The impact of Paul's evangelism was of such a magnitude that when he arrived at Thessalonica, the unbelieving Jews cried out in alarm, "These that have turned the world upside down are come hither also!"[2]

But Paul, besides being an apostle and a missionary, was also a prophet. Much of what we know about the Second Appearing of Christ and the resurrection of the believers has come to us from his pen.

Millions of bereaved believers have drawn comfort and hope from Paul's prophetic assurance, "the dead in Christ shall rise first."[3]

Thousands of Christian martyrs have faced the searing flames or the tearing fangs and claws of savage beasts with their voices raised in songs of hope—the hope that came to them through Paul's prophecy, ". . . the Lord himself shall descend from heaven with a shout, with the voice of the archangel, and the trump of God: . . . we . . . shall be caught up together with them in the clouds, to meet the Lord in the air: and so shall we ever be with the Lord. Wherefore comfort one another with these words."[4]

Probably drawing from Joshua's experience with the five kings of Canaan,[5] Paul prophetically illustrated the final conquest of Satan by the people of God, "And the God of peace shall bruise Satan under your feet shortly."[6]

In his classic argument for the resurrection, Paul repeatedly insisted with beautiful logic that the future resurrection of believers was certain—as certain as was the historical fact of Christ's own resurrection.[7] But after all arguments had been presented and logic had been exhausted, the apostle gave that majestic prophecy of the believer's destiny, "Behold, I shew you a mystery; We shall not all sleep [die], but we shall all be changed, in a moment, in the twinkling of an eye, at the last trump: for the trumpet shall sound, and the dead shall be raised incorruptible, and we shall be changed."[8]

The prophet Paul sounded a more somber note when he revealed the future to his beloved spiritual son, Timothy. He warned of impending departure from the faith and the growth of spiritism and devil worship. He predicted that honesty would become a lost virtue and men would develop an immunity to the voice of conscience.[9] Later in his life Paul wrote another letter to Timothy. Again his message assumed a prophetic note as he revealed to Timothy that in the end days perilous times would come with men majoring in pride, egotism, greed, ingratitude and blasphemy. He told Timothy about the generation gap and the total breakdown in loyalties. He warned that even in Christian circles worship would consist of nothing but form and ritual without power or reality.[10] With the perceptive eye of prophecy Paul foresaw the day when the nominal Christian church would reject conservative theology and would secure pastors who would preach what their congregations wanted to hear.[11]

It is fitting that Paul's final letter should end with a personal prophetic message. His service for Christ had meant blood and sweat and toil and tears. And now he was arriving at the end of the road—for him it would be Caesar's sword. His autobiography is dramatically simple: "I have fought a good fight, I have finished my course, I have kept the faith . . . I am now ready to be offered, and the time of my departure is at hand."[12]

What a beautiful way to end a career! But that was not the end. Paul had one more thing to say, and it was prophetic. "Henceforth there is laid up for me a crown of righteousness, which the Lord, the righteous judge, shall give me at that day." Previously he had admitted to "having a desire to depart, and to be with Christ; which is far better."[13]

The apostle James gives to us only one brief prophetic statement. He exhorts the brethren to wait patiently for the coming of the Lord and then assures them that the Lord's return was drawing near.[14]

Jude also confines his exercise of the prophetic gift to one warning, that in the end times mockers would appear who would walk after their own lusts, encourage divisions, live sensually and be devoid of the Holy Spirit.[15]

In Peter's first letter he refers to the coming revelation of Jesus Christ and to the incorruptible and undefiled inheritance that is reserved in heaven for God's dear children.[16]

In his Second Epistle, Peter gives several striking prophetic warnings concerning the end times and the end of all time. He warned against false teachers who would bring into the church damnable heresies, even going so far as to deny the Lord that bought them.[17] But Peter's most dramatic warning is to be found in his closing chapter where he exposes the spiritual stupidity of those who deny the validity of the prophetic Scriptures. He labels them as scoffers who walk after their own lusts and are willfully ignorant.[18] Then Peter provides the most detailed prophetic account of the final dissolution of heaven and earth to be found in the Bible.[19] It is a grim picture indeed. But before Peter closes his prophetic message, he adds a thrilling note of hope and triumph for the child of God, "Nevertheless we, according to his promise, look for new heavens and a new earth, wherein dwelleth righteousness . . . be diligent that ye may be found of him in peace, without spot, and blameless."[20]

The title, Prince of New Testament Prophets, must be reserved for the apostle John. Through him the Holy Spirit gave to us that amazing Revelation of Jesus Christ—the only totally prophetic book in the New Testament. But John's prophecies were not confined to this one book. In his First Epistle he warned that the world would pass away with its lusts[21] and that Antichrist would appear and would be characterized by a denial of the Father and the Son.[22]

John shared with Paul that blessed hope of Christ's Second Appearing and assured his children in the faith that when that happens we shall be like Him and we will see Him as He is.[23] He also reminded them that the possession of this hope demands and produces purity of life.[24]

In his Second Epistle, John identifies those who deny the unique deity of Jesus Christ as deceivers and antichrists.[25] Five times in his first two Epistles John mentions the Antichrist. Why? Probably because of the deep convictions John held regarding the incarnation and deity of Jesus. And knowing that the Antichrist will deny that deity, he became in the eyes of John the embodiment of all that is vile and evil and Satanic.

It was on the lovely island of Patmos that John reached the pinnacle of achievement. It was not by accident that he was designated the disciple "whom Jesus loved."[26] He had earned it. Only John accompanied Jesus into the judgment hall of the high priest.[27] And of all the twelve disciples, only John was found at the cross and received the commission to care for the mother of Jesus.[28] All this may have played a part in the choice of John to be the recipient of the majestic, mysterious, exciting and understandable, as well as baffling book of the Revelation.

Footnotes

1. Acts 19:10
2. Acts 17:6
3. I Thessalonians 4:16
4. I Thessalonians 4:16-18
5. Joshua 10:24
6. Romans 16:20
7. I Corinthians 15:20-22
8. I Corinthians 15:51,52
9. I Timothy 4:1-3
10. II Timothy 3:1-5
11. II Timothy 4:3
12. II Timothy 4:7,6
13. II Timothy 4:8; Philippians 1:23
14. James 5:7,8
15. Jude 18,19
16. I Peter 1:13,4
17. II Peter 2:1-3
18. II Peter 3:1-9
19. II Peter 3:10-12
20. II Peter 3:13,14
21. I John 2:17
22. I John 2:18,19

23. I John 3:2
24. I John 3:3
25. II John 7
26. John 13:23
27. John 18:15,16
28. John 19:26.27

CHAPTER 5

Signs and Sounds

The Olivet Discourse of Jesus, with its "signs of the times," is built around three questions asked by Jesus' disciples.

1. When shall these things be?
2. What shall be the sign of Thy coming?
3. What shall be the sign of the end of the world?

They asked no question about the future destiny of the Church because at that time it still was the mystery of the ages, concealed from both prophets and angels.[1] The Church would be born at the death and resurrection of Christ and would take its first breath of life at Pentecost.

The first question remained unanswered. He

merely said, "But of that day and hour knoweth no man, no, not the angels of heaven, but my Father only."[2] This is very significant. It means that when any person attempts to establish a prophetic timetable, he is accusing Christ of not being truthful.

In the Authorized Version of the Bible, the term, "signs of the times" is used only once.[3] As generally used in the New Testament, the word "signs" refers to miraculous demonstrations of divine power in the physical and natural realms.

In studying the "signs of the times," it is important to remember that none of these refers to the Second *Appearing* of Christ for the Church. They cover three major crises: The destruction of Jerusalem and the Temple; The Second Coming of Christ; and The Day of the Lord.

Most of the "signs of the times" refer to the Second Coming of Christ at the close of the Great Tribulation.

The signs that Jesus gave come under eleven classifications. Then in Revelation John gives an additional sign, making a total of twelve.

1. *The Jerusalem sign*—in two phases. The first was the prophecy dealing with the destruction of Jerusalem by the Romans in A.D. 70, and the sign of that tragedy was its encompassment by Titus' army.[4] The second phase was the release of Jerusalem from Gentile governments and this was fulfilled during the 1967 six-day war. It was this remarkable fulfillment that indicated the times of the Gentiles have come to an end.[5]

2. *Celestial signs*—preceding the Second Coming of Christ. These will consist of alarming disturb-

ances involving the sun, moon and stars. For centuries men have steered their ships and checked their time by the infallible, unchanging course of the heavenly bodies. But as the end of the age draws near, to the terror of men, the planetary system will go out of control and become an instrument of judgment.[6]

3. *Atmospheric signs*—indicated in Luke's account of the Olivet Discourse. Here "the sea and the waves roaring"[7] suggest violent winds and storms of uprecedented severity.

4. *Geological signs*—"earthquakes, in divers places."[8] As the coming of Christ approaches we can expect to see disastrous earthquake and volcanic action in areas previously untouched by these catastrophes. Hardly a week goes by without the news media reporting earthquakes somewhere in the world. Our scientists are presently much concerned about the development of hot spots on the slopes of some of our western volcanoes. They are no longer talking about *if* there will be a major earthquake in Southern California, but rather *when* it will come. Most of them agree that it is long overdue.

5. *Biological signs*—". . . there shall be . . . pestilences."[9] We must ever be grateful for the advances made by science in conquering or controlling various diseases. But a very strange thing is happening—germs and viruses are developing an immunity to antibiotics. The same thing is true of destructive insects in their reaction to insecticides. Science can put men on the moon but has yet to find a cure for the common cold. Malignancy and

cardiac diseases remain the fearful dragons of destruction. It is probable that as we continue our journey through the end times, new plagues and epidemics, previously unknown to medical science, will depopulate vast areas.

6. *Social signs* have within the last several decades reared their ugly heads of violence. Jesus prophesied that " . . . the brother shall deliver up the brother to death, and the father the child: *and the children shall rise up against their parents,* . . ."[10] History is repeating itself and the same attitudes that caused man to lose his knowledge of God are becoming increasingly prevalent today—with "vile affections" but "without *natural* affection."[11] The alarming increase in the divorce rate, abortions, infanticides and violent crimes—all these indicate a frightening trend toward a culture without feeling, affection or conscience. Racial violence, industrial strife, militant demonstrations and organizations all play their bloody part in the fulfillment of the social signs of the times.

7. *Moral signs* were stated both by Jesus and the apostle Paul as indicative of the end times. Jesus said, "As it was in the days of Noe [Noah], so shall it be also in the days of the Son of man. They did eat, they drank, they married wives, they were given in marriage, until the day that Noe [Noah] entered into the ark, and the flood came, and destroyed them all."[12] Many Bible teachers feel that these verses do not refer to ordinary eating, drinking and marrying but rather to extreme gluttony, drunkenness and promiscuous sexual practices.

Along with other contemporary freedoms, the

world boasts of its "new morality" which is, of course, no morality. Sex is the trade mark of today's culture. From the silver screen, billboards, magazines and newspaper ads, comics (?), the TV and pornographic magazines there comes a constant stream of sub-bestial filth.

Paul had in mind the same moral diseases when he wrote, "For of this sort are they which creep into houses, and lead captive silly women laden with sins, led away with divers lusts."[13]

The current trend toward permissiveness in matters of moral conduct, along with recent decisions of the high courts regarding pornography, promises an abundant harvest of venereal diseases and degeneration that will surpass the vilest chapters of human history.

8. *Religious signs* began to manifest themselves even while the apostle John was living. In Christ's message to the Laodicean church its members were accused of being lukewarm, proud, wretched, miserable, poor, blind and naked.[14] Even the best of the churches of Asia, the Ephesian church, had already lost its first love.[15]

Jesus prophesied that false teachers and false christs would arise and deceive many.[16] He warned that iniquity would abound and the love of many would wax cold.[17] As Christ looked ahead to the days preceding His return He saw how both faith and faithfulness would decline—how even Christians would trust God only when there was nothing else to do. In deep pathos He asked the searching question, "When the Son of man cometh, shall he find faith on the earth?"[18]

It is not likely that Jesus was referring to personal faith here, but rather to *the* faith—the entire body of truth delivered unto the saints. Jesus foresaw the coming of apostasies and heresies—the evil malignancy of liberal theology to be followed by more subtle, but equally deadly, neo-orthodoxy. He saw the creeping paralysis of materialism and worldliness slowly inactivating the spiritual nerve centers of the church, until worship in Spirit and in truth would be almost obsolete.

9. *Political signs* are described by Jesus as ". . . wars and rumours of wars . . . nation shall rise against nation, and kingdom against kingdom[19] . . . distress of nations, with perplexity."[20]

League of Nations, Geneva Conference, United Nations—one after another these human institutions of peace have demonstrated the futility of man's efforts to eliminate wars and produce universal peace. The nations of the world have two problems. They have forgotten God, and they are wicked. And God said, "The wicked shall be turned into hell, and all the nations that forget God."[21] "There is no peace, saith the Lord, unto the wicked."[22] And since man cannot eliminate or legislate the innate hostility from his nature, there will continue to be "wars and rumours of wars" until the Prince of Peace comes to establish His kingdom of equity and righteousness.

During the Tribulation there will be a supreme effort to establish a federation of governments, and this will for a limited time meet with considerable success.[23] But eventually the King of the South, probably representing the united Arab world, will attack the Antichrist's federation and blood will again be spilled.[24]

The prophets do not paint an optimistic picture of future world politics. Graft and deceit will grow on the local level. International intrigue and tensions will increase. Taxes will continue to rise. Inflation will assume such proportions that a man's daily wage will be barely enough to buy essential food. "A measure [one quart] of wheat for a penny [a day's wage], and [or] three measures [quarts] of barley [cattle food] for a penny [a day's wage]."[25]

10. *Evangelistic sign*—Jesus said that "this gospel of the kingdom shall be preached in all the world for a witness unto all nations; and then shall the end come."[26]

Never since the birth of the Christian church has so much wealth, so much talent and ability and so many people been dedicated to the fulfillment of the Great Commission.[27] Medical, educational, vocational, linguistic and technological science have united in a supreme effort to fulfill this prophecy. Through evangelical churches and many independent organizations and through the use of the most modern techniques known to science the Gospel of the Lord Jesus Christ is being carried into every nation on earth.

11. *The Jerusalem sign* has been referred to previously but it deserves more attention. Jesus prophesied of the inhabitants of Jerusalem that they "shall be led away captive into all nations: and Jerusalem shall be trodden down of the Gentiles, until the times of the Gentiles be fulfilled."[28] Prior to the 1967 six-day war, the most ardent student of

biblical prophecy would not have dared to predict the fulfillment of this prophecy within the forseeable future. The Jordanian forces were securely entrenched on their side of no man's land. Never, under any circumstance would they yield one foot of territory to the hated Zionists. And that determination was backed up by the might of Egyptian and Syrian forces and Russian equipment. But God the Almighty intervened! In an interview with Teddy Kollek, the distinguished mayor of Jerusalem said to me as we discussed the liberation of Jerusalem, "God fought on our side."

12. *The Ecology sign* is well concealed in a statement recorded by the apostle John. "And the nations were angry, and thy wrath is come, and the time of the dead, that they should be judged, and that thou shouldest give reward unto thy servants the prophets, and to the saints, and them that fear thy name, small and great; and shouldest *destroy them which destroy the earth.*"[29] Water pollution, air pollution, soil pollution—man in his greed and selfishness seems to be possessed by an insane urge to "destroy the earth." Smog smothers and hastens the death of millions who dwell in the great metropolises. The beautiful verdant valleys and hills of Virginia, Pennsylvania and other states are left with hideous scars by the operators of strip mining. No amount of skin grafting will ever restore their original beauty. Motorists, with wicked thoughtlessness, scatter bottles and cans along our highways. The pleasure of walking barefooted along many of our beaches will soon be rendered hazardous because

of the sharp fragments of broken bottles thrown on the sand by "earth destroyers."

It is no longer difficult to understand or question God's motives in causing this earth to pass away and bringing into existence a new heaven and a new earth. The old heaven has been defiled by Satan,[30] and the old earth is being destroyed by depraved man.

THE SOUNDS of biblical prophecy, as well as the signs, are of special interest to believers. Paul informed us that at the Second Appearing of Christ, the Lord Himself will descend from heaven with *a shout,* with *the voice of the archangel* and *the trump of God.*[31] Here we have three sounds which will announce the fulfillment of that blessed hope of the church. And we will hear all three! What Christ will shout . . . what the archangel will say . . . and the note that the trump will sound, we do not know. But it will all be good and glorious! These will be the most thrilling, the most exciting and the most glorious sounds that human ears have ever heard. We will hear the voice of our blessed Lord, and then in a moment, in the twinkling of an eye we will be like Him for we shall see Him face to face—as He is!

But there was another sound prophesied through John's pen. It is the sound of the voice of the Holy Spirit as He joins with the bride, the Church, in praying, "Come." "And the Spirit and the bride say, Come."[32] And both the Spirit and every true child of God who loves the appearing of our Lord Jesus Christ, say longingly and lovingly, "Even so, come, Lord Jesus."[33]

Footnotes

1. I Peter 1:11,12
2. Matthew 24:36
3. Matthew 16:3
4. Luke 21:20-23
5. Luke 21:24
6. Mark 13:24,25
7. Luke 21:25
8. Matthew 24:7
9. Matthew 24:7; Luke 21:11
10. Matthew 10:21
11. Romans 1:26,31
12. Luke 17:26,27; Matthew 24:37-39
13. II Timothy 3:6
14. Revelation 3:16,17
15. Revelation 2:4
16. Mark 13:22; I John 4:1
17. Matthew 24:12
18. Luke 18:8
19. Matthew 24:6,7
20. Luke 21:25
21. Psalm 9:17
22. Isaiah 48:22
23. Revelation 17:12
24. Daniel 11:40
25. Revelation 6:5,6
26. Matthew 24:14
27. Matthew 28:19,20
28. Luke 21:24
29. Revelation 11:18

30. Revelation 12:10
31. I Thessalonians 4:16
32. Revelation 22:17
33. Revelation 22:20

CHAPTER 6

That Blessed Hope

Jesus *is* coming! He said He would. The early Christians lived and died in that hope. The apostles wrote about it. We believe it is imminent. We pray for it to happen. When Jesus does come for the Church, what will that event mean to us? For those living at that time it will mean many wonderful things.

It will mean the end of conflict with the flesh, the world and Satan. From the moment of our spiritual birth we are engaged in conflict with these evil forces. The Word of God never promised that the Christian life would consist of a delightful residency on cloud nine. The new convert soon discovers that we wrestle against "powers, against the rulers of the darkness of this world, against spiritual wickedness in high places."[1] Too many believers spend miserable years attempting to escape from the frustrating experience described by Paul, ". . . the good that I would I do not: but the evil which I would not, that I do . . . I delight in the law of God after the inward man: but I see another law in my members, warring against the law of my mind, and bringing me into captivity to the law of sin which is in my members. O wretched man that I am! who shall deliver me from the body of this death?"[2] This type of experience will be gone forever when Jesus appears.

The Second Appearing of Christ will mean emancipation from temptation. When we see Jesus, instantly "we shall be like him; for we shall see him as he is."[3] Our human nature of sin will not be found in our glorified bodies. This internal source of temptation will no longer exist. James wrote of it, "Every man is tempted, when he is drawn away of his own lust, and enticed."[4] Also, Christ's appearing will take us from this world and all areas of Satan's influence so these sources of temptation will be removed. Imagine what it will be like never to be tempted to become angry, or resentful, or dishonest, or lustful, or envious!

When Christ appears it will mean release from sorrow and disappointments. There will be no heartaches or tears in glory. The tensions and griefs of life will be forever past. Redeemed parents will never again weep over wayward children. No

Christian wives will shed bitter tears over God-hating husbands. Since we will know as we are known, understanding everything as God does, there will be no grief. Emotional storms will never arise. Depressions and moods will no longer torment. There will be peace of mind and soul and happiness supreme.

When Christ appears it will mean a happy reunion. Those who are alive at that glorious moment will not precede those who are dead in Christ. In fact, "the dead in Christ shall rise first: *then* we which are alive and remain shall be caught up together with them in the clouds, to meet the Lord in the air."[5] Our fellow believers who have been taken from us by death will be restored. What a family reunion that will be! Husbands and wives, parents and children, mothers and babies—all will be joyfully reunited!

Will we recognize each other? Of course we will. The powers of death and the glory of the resurrection will not destroy identity. The two men who appeared with Jesus on the Mount of Transfiguration were definitely recognized as Moses and Elijah. Peter even offered to build sacred tents for them and referred to them by name.[6]

When the two disciples met the resurrected Lord on the road to Emmaus, they would have recognized Him immediately, "But their eyes were holden that they should not know him."[7]

When Christ appears it will mean an end to all physical infirmities. There will be no malignancies. Those who had been blind will see. The lame will walk without limping. The maimed will be whole.

The deaf will hear and the dumb will speak. The agony of arthritis will be gone. The poet said,

"The old will be young there forever,
Transformed in a moment of time.
Immortal we'll stand in His likeness,
The stars and the sun to outshine."[8]

Yes, there will be no sickness and no death when we stand in His likeness! Then we will join Paul in singing that triumphant resurrection refrain

"Death is swallowed up in victory.
O death, where is thy sting?
O grave, where is thy victory?
But thanks be to God, which giveth us the victory
Through our Lord Jesus Christ."[9]

When Christ appears it will mean a transforming meeting. So many times there has risen from our hearts the song of hope,

"Face to face shall I behold Him,
Far beyond the starry sky.
Face to face in all His glory
I shall see Him by-and-by."[10]

But when Jesus finally appears, hope will become reality! We shall look upon the face of our wonderful Lord who loved us and gave Himself for us. No longer will we see through a glass darkly but face to face! And when we shall see that dear, precious face something will happen to us—suddenly we will be like Him—exactly like Him! All the weaknesses, failures, wanderings and frustrations of life will be gone! No wonder the man of God wrote, "I will behold thy face in righteousness: I shall be satisfied, when I awake, with thy likeness."[11]

The Second Appearing of Christ will mean an

amazing physical change. The apostle Paul wrote, ". . . we shall all be changed, in a moment, in the twinkling of an eye."[12] Then he added in another letter, "We look for the Saviour, the Lord Jesus Christ: who shall change our vile body, that it may be fashioned like unto his glorious body."[13] In that great resurrection chapter, First Corinthians fifteen, the apostle provides considerable detail regarding the glorified body of the believer. It will be an incorruptible body. We begin to die from the moment of birth. The process of decay will not be present in eternity.[14]

Our new body will be glorious, free from all causes of dishonor and embarrassment.[15]

When we meet Jesus we will discover that our new body will have powers and abilities we never dreamed possible.[16] Time, space and matter will no longer be deterrents to our desires. Just as the resurrected Jesus entered the room where the "doors were shut [locked] . . . for fear of the Jews,"[17] so there will be no material barriers to our glorified body.

We will have a "spiritual" body, one that shall "also bear the image of the heavenly."[18] In other words, our new body will be just like His body—that of our wonderful, wonderful Lord. Blessedly, gloriously, wonderfully—we shall be like Jesus when we shall see Him as He is.

Footnotes

1. Ephesians 6:12
2. Romans 7:19, 22-24
3. I John 3:2
4. James 1:14
5. I Thessalonians 4:16,17
6. Matthew 17:1-4
7. Luke 24:16
8. Mrs. A. Lehman
9. I Corinthians 15:54-57
10. Fanny Crosby
11. Psalm 17:15
12. I Corinthians 15:51,52
13. Philippians 3:20,21
14. I Corinthians 15:42
15. I Corinthians 15:43
16. I Corinthians 15:43
17. John 20:19
18. I Corinthians 15:44,49

CHAPTER 7

The Leading Characters

As this age draws to a close, there will appear upon the stage of human events four leading characters, each playing his major role—three of them of a sinister nature and the last one bringing in the golden finale of eternal joy and glory. Minor parts will be played by many stars and extras, but the spotlight of prophecy focuses on the four leading characters. Several of these have been referred to previously.

SATAN

Behind the generation, the social, the racial, the industrial and all other tragic people-dividing gaps, leading every violent demonstration on the streets or on the campuses, fomenting every bloody war and every advance of communism, there lurks the archenemy of God and man, Satan. He is not a figment of imagination nor is he merely an evil, negative principle. Satan is a live, incredibly intelligent, unbelievably powerful and totally evil creature. He is completely dedicated to an attempt to thwart God's benevolent designs and interfere with the fulfillment of His eternal plan of the ages.

Satan writes and produces the shows put on by the criminals, the crime syndicates and the war lords. The Antichrist and the False Prophet will be taking leading parts in the final drama but their skill and power will be Satanic in origin.[1]

His Origin

There are two Bible references which are believed to throw light upon the origin of Satan. The first of these comes to us from the inspired pen of Isaiah.[2] He pictures Satan as having been originally Lucifer, star of the morning. Ezekiel throws additional light upon Satan's original position as the prophet uses the king of Tyrus as an indirect means of addressing Satan.[3] Lucifer is described as the sum total of wisdom, beauty and perfection. He was in Eden, the garden of God. He was the embodiment of harmony and everything beautiful and pleasant. He was anointed as the superior of all other angelic beings. He walked upon the holy mountain of God and up and down in the midst of the stones of fire.

It is apparent that angels were created by God as

free moral agents. Jude, in his Epistle, refers to angels, "which kept not their first estate, but left their own habitation, he hath reserved in everlasting chains under darkness unto the judgment of the great day."[4] Peter also wrote about "angels that sinned."[5] So in the eternal ages past there came a time when Lucifer, exercising his free moral agency, sounded the cry of rebellion and treason, "I will exalt my throne above the stars of God: I will sit also upon the mount of the congregation, in the sides of the north: I will ascend above the heights of the clouds; I will be like the most High."[6] Ezekiel describes that tragic decision in the words, ". . . iniquity was found in thee."[7]

Some Bible students believe that one third of the angelic creation joined Lucifer in his act of treason, basing this belief on John's statement that "the great red dragon . . . his tail drew the third part of the stars of heaven, and did cast them to the earth."[8]

We next see Satan assuming or inhabiting the form of a serpent, seducing Eve and persuading her to doubt God's goodness and veracity, thus bringing the curse upon humanity and the creation.[9]

He successfully tempted David to take a forbidden census of Israel which led to the death of thousands of innocent victims of David's pride.[10]

In that strange book of Job we have the record of Satan twice reporting his activities to God, suggesting that he is obligated to do this on a regular basis.[11]

Prior to the public ministry of Jesus Christ, He met Satan in open conflict in the wilderness of temptation. Again and again Satan launched his fierce attacks against Jesus on the mountain and on top of the temple only to be met by the sword of the Spirit, the Word of God skillfully wielded by Jesus.[12]

The New Testament describes Satan's activities as taking away the Word of God when it is sown in the hearts of men;[13] binding God's children with infirmities and disabilities;[14] persuading people to lie in matters of business[15] and leading Christians into mortal compromise.[16]

John informs us that Satan is constantly engaged in accusing the believers,[17] and this explains why it is necessary for us to have an Advocate with the Father, Jesus Christ the righteous.[18]

After the Second Coming of Christ and the battle of Armageddon, Satan will be bound and cast into the bottomless pit for the duration of Christ's Millennial reign.[19] At the close of that period, Satan will be freed and will lead the final human rebellion against the authority of God.[20] Of course, he will be defeated, his armies will be destroyed by fire and Satan will be cast into the lake of fire, and "shall be tormented day and night for ever and ever."[21]

THE ANTICHRIST

The title "Antichrist" is peculiar to the Epistles of John. Even in his Revelation John did not use this title, but referred to this champion of Satan as "a beast."[22] As previously mentioned, the apostle Paul called him "that man of sin . . . the son of perdition . . . the mystery of iniquity . . . that Wicked."[23] Some people have tied Paul's term, "the son of perdition," with Jesus' use of the same term as applied to

Judas[24] and have therefore concluded that Judas will be the Antichrist. That this cannot be true is evident from John's description of the Beast in Revelation thirteen and seventeen.

The apostle Paul intimates that the Antichrist may be living somewhere on earth prior to the Second Appearing of Christ but will not be able to reveal his true identity until after the Holy Spirit and the Church have been removed from the earth.[25] There can be no doubt that the increase in witchcraft, spiritism, astrology, fortune-telling and the occults, including devil worship, is setting the stage for the debut of that Man of Sin. TV shows and movies depicting witchcraft, supermen, monsters and apparitions are conditioning the imaginations of children and youth to accept and believe without question the miracles the Antichrist will perform when he is revealed in his true character.[26]

In describing him, the Bible indicates that he will establish a ten-nation confederacy,[27] having the same characteristics as the three empires which preceded the Roman Empire—the lightning conquest of Greece, the tenacity of Persia and the inhumanity of the Babylonians.[28] It may indeed be prophetically significant that only recently the Common Market of Europe reached the prophetic figure of ten nations. The move from economic unity to political unity is not outside the realm of possibility!

The Antichrist is pictured as promoting worship of the devil, making dynamic speeches, blasphemously speaking against God, making war with the saints, having power over all nations and demanding universal worship.[29] He will make a covenant with the nation of Israel promising seven years of protection and freedom of worship. But after three and one half years he will break this agreement, outlaw the Jewish ceremonial worship and declare himself as God.[30] Isaiah calls this agreement "a covenant with death, and with hell."[31]

At the end of the Great Tribulation he will assemble the armies of earth to engage in combat with Christ who has come to the Mount of Olives with His saints.[32] His troops will be "slain with the sword of him that sat upon the horse, which sword proceeded out of his mouth: and all the fowls were filled with their flesh."[33] The prophet John wrote, "And the beast was taken . . . and . . . cast alive into a lake of fire burning with brimstone."[34]

The identity of the Antichrist is not so much a mystery as a challenge. It provides us with the only numerical puzzle to be found in the Bible. I wonder if John did not chuckle a bit when he wrote, "Here is wisdom. Let him that hath understanding count the number of the beast: for it is the number of a man; and his number is Six hundred threescore and six."[35] But John gives more definite information concerning the Beast's identity. He writes of ". . . his deadly wound,"[36] and that all the world wondered (with amazement) after him. He will be able to accomplish superhuman feats—to be *the* authentic Super Man!

Continuing his identification of the Antichrist, John informed us that at the time he wrote the book of Revelation, the Antichrist was not then living but *had been living before that time!* The apostle goes on to add, "And there are seven kings: five are fallen [dead], and one is [then living at John's time], and the other is not yet come [not yet living at John's time]; and when he cometh, he must continue a short space [a brief reign]. And the beast that was [prior to John's time], and is not [dead at John's time], even he is the eighth [this is the Antichrist], and is of the seven [one of the seven great rulers], and goeth into perdition [will be cast alive into the lake of fire]."[37]

Were we to take this literally, it would mean that the Antichrist will be one of the five important rulers who had reigned prior to John's Patmos experience. Some students of prophecy believe that Satan will be permitted to imitate the incarnation of Jesus Christ and that the Antichrist will be the product of this imitation. Other students believe that he will be one of the former Roman rulers who will be resurrected to serve Satan's evil purpose. Many Bible teachers take John's identification of the Beast symbolically rather than literally.

THE FALSE PROPHET

In telling us about this High Priest of the Antichrist, John writes that he saw him "coming up out of the earth; and he had two horns like a lamb, and he spake as a dragon."[38] This suggests a treacherous and deceitful character who can be docile and flattering when the occasion demands it but can be equally ruthless and cruel to serve his own purpose.

The False Prophet, receiving his authority and

power from the Beast, will enforce universal worship of him. At the beginning of their reign they will be endorsed by the World Church[39] and will support and protect this super church. But when their reign is firmly established the mask of cooperation will be removed and they will eliminate the religious institution,[40] proclaim that the Beast is the only true god and demand that he be worshiped under penalty of starvation and later, execution.[41]

To support his claim of deity for the Beast, the False Prophet will perform miracles and great wonders, bringing fire down from heaven in the sight of men. He will also construct a statue of the Antichrist and be able to give life to it so that it will both speak and cause to be killed all those who will not worship it.[42]

But his power will come to an end. The False Prophet will join with the Beast in his attack upon Jesus Christ at the battle of Armageddon. He, along with the Antichrist, will be taken and thrown alive into the lake of fire.[43]

THE LORD JESUS CHRIST

The fourth and principal character in the drama of the end times is the Lord Jesus Christ. Much more will be said about Him later. For the moment let us look at Him through the adoring eyes of John, the loving apostle.

"I saw . . . the Son of man, clothed with a garment down to the foot, and girt about the paps with a golden girdle. His head and his hairs were white like wool, as white as snow; and his eyes were as a flame of fire; and his feet like unto fine brass, as if they burned in a furnace; and his voice as the sound of many waters . . . his countenance was as the sun shineth in his strength . . . [He] is the faithful witness, and the first begotten of the dead, and the prince of the kings of the earth."[44]

And our response to this gaze? The same as that of John, "Unto him that loved us, and washed us from our sins in his own blood, and hath made us kings and priests unto God and his Father; to him be glory and dominion for ever and ever. Amen."[45]

Footnotes

1. Revelation 13:2
2. Isaiah 14:12-15
3. Ezekiel 28:12-15
4. Jude 6
5. II Peter 2:4
6. Isaiah 14:13,14
7. Ezekiel 28:15
8. Revelation 12:4,9
9. Genesis 3:1-19
10. I Chronicles 21:1
11. Job 1:6; 2:1
12. Matthew 4:1-11
13. Mark 4:15
14. Luke 13:16
15. Acts 5:3
16. I Corinthians 7:5
17. Revelation 12:10
18. I John 2:1

19. Revelation 20:1-3
20. Revelation 20:7-9
21. Revelation 20:10
22. Revelation 11:7; 13:1
23. II Thessalonians 2:3,7,8
24. John 17:12
25. II Thessalonians 2:7,8
26. Revelation 13:13,14
27. Revelation 13:1
28. Revelation 13:2; Daniel 7:4-6
29. Revelation 13:4-8
30. Daniel 7:27; Revelation 13:12
31. Isaiah 28:15
32. Revelation 19:19
33. Revelation 19:21
34. Revelation 19:20
35. Revelation 13:18
36. Revelation 13:3,12
37. Revelation 17:10,11
38. Revelation 13:11
39. Revelation 17:1-7
40. Revelation 17:16-18
41. Revelation 13:7,17,15
42. Revelation 13:13-15
43. Revelation 19:20
44. Revelation 1:12-16,5
45. Revelation 1:5,6

CHAPTER 8

The Metropolis of Prophecy

Every student of God's Word should have an opportunity to visit the lands of the Bible. To follow the steps of Moses through Egypt and stand in awe before the mighty pyramids and other great monuments so closely related in time to the Bible, adds a new dimension to biblical history.

But the supreme thrill is to be experienced in walking through the streets of Jerusalem where with every step the visitor treads upon history and prophecy.

Jerusalem is the most interesting and the most important city in the world. Greater and larger cities have towered in all their glory and might in ages past but now exist only as crumbling ruins. Tourists by the thousands visit the sites of Petra, Jerash, Baalbek, Corinth, Babylon, Nineveh and Memphis and find nothing but the *dead* remains of a glorious past. But in Jerusalem they discover the *living* remains of an illustrious past and the promise of an even more glorious future.

Jerusalem is an ancient city. In Abraham's time it was known as Salem (the city of peace), and was ruled by that mysterious biblical character, Melchizedek, honored by the Bible as being greater than Abraham.[1] This was a site of sacred memories to Abraham until the day of his death. According to tradition, it was here that he bound his beloved son Isaac and prepared to offer him as a sacrifice to God. And what a blessed memory—that ram that God provided as a substitute![2]

Jerusalem became the capital of the united kingdom of Israel under King David,[3] and he purchased here the site for the later erection of the temple by his son, Solomon.[4]

It was here that Jesus, as a babe, was presented to the Lord as the first-born son of Mary,[5] and later, at the age of twelve He was found, "sitting in the midst of the doctors, both hearing them, and asking them questions. And all that heard him were astonished at his understanding and answers."[6]

Christ made His triumphant entry into the city of Jerusalem. Its streets rang with the loud hosannas of the multitude as they acclaimed Him as ". . . the King that cometh in the name of the Lord."[7]

It was here that Jesus was nationally rejected as Sovereign and Messiah in favor of Caesar and

Barabbas,[8] and then was crucified in fulfillment of prophecy.[9] Hours later, Christ was forsaken by His Father as He bore our sins in His own body upon the tree.[10]

Christians will always remember Jerusalem as the site of the two cornerstones of our faith—the resurrection of Jesus Christ[11] and the coming of the Holy Spirit in great power upon the disciples.[12]

Most biblical prophecies focus upon the person of Jesus Christ and upon the geographical site of Jerusalem. The Temple will be rebuilt here and sacrificial worship will be restored.[13] When the Antichrist breaks his covenant with the Jews, he will sit "in the temple of God, shewing himself that he is God."[14] John also refers to the Temple existing during the Great Tribulation.[15] Rumors continue to persist that stones are being cut and other materials are being purchased and stored so that all will be in readiness for the reconstruction of the Temple.

I questioned Jerusalem mayor Teddy Kollek about this rumor. He attempted to evade the question, and with his usual hearty laugh he said, "Oh, we don't have to worry about that. When the time comes, the New Jerusalem with its Temple and everything else will come down from heaven. Isn't that what your New Testament says?"

It is at Jerusalem that the Antichrist will sign that evil seven-year covenant with the Jews[16] only to break it three and one half years later by setting up in the Temple the living image of himself.[17]

Jerusalem has known many bitter and dark days. It has been destroyed five times and in the course of its history it has changed hands more than twenty times. When destroyed by Titus in A.D. 70, 600,000 Jews were slaughtered in the city alone—the total in the nation was over one million. More than 100,000 were sold into slavery, another fulfillment of prophecy.[18] Later, Hadrian had plows drawn over the site of Jerusalem and he established a Roman colony on a near-by location.

Jerusalem will suffer its final tragedy when it will be invaded and occupied by the Antichrist and his troops. The prophet Zechariah paints a grim picture of that coming disaster. "I will gather all nations against Jerusalem to battle; and the city shall be taken, and the houses rifled, and the women ravished; and half of the city shall go forth into captivity."[19]

In their desperate plight, the Jews will cry to God for deliverance, and Christ will come to the Mount of Olives. When the Jews see and recognize Him, they will experience a great spiritual awakening.[20] The national revival that will follow is pictured by the prophet in glowing terms. "And I will pour upon the house of David, and upon the inhabitants of Jerusalem, the spirit of grace and of supplications: and they shall look upon me whom they have pierced, and they shall mourn for him, as one mourneth for his only son, and shall be in bitterness for him, as one that is in bitterness for his firstborn.[21] . . . And one shall say unto him, What are these wounds in thine hands? Then he shall answer, Those with which I was wounded in the house of my friends."[22]

The establishing of Jerusalem as the religious and political capital of the world is a favorite theme of the Old Testament prophets.

"So shall ye know that I am the Lord your God dwelling in Zion, my holy mountain: then shall Jerusalem be holy.[23] . . . Judah shall dwell for ever, and Jerusalem from generation to generation. For I will cleanse their blood that I have not cleansed: for the Lord dwelleth in Zion."[24]

"Behold, I create Jerusalem a rejoicing, and her people a joy. And I will rejoice in Jerusalem, and joy in my people: and the voice of weeping shall be no more heard in her, nor the voice of crying. There shall be no more thence an infant of days, nor an old man that hath not filled his days: for the child shall die an hundred years old; but the sinner being an hundred years old shall be accursed."[25]

"Jerusalem shall be inhabited as towns without walls for the multitude of men and cattle therein: for I, saith the Lord, will be unto her a wall of fire round about, and will be the glory in the midst of her."[26]

Yes, the directional arrows of biblical prophecy are aimed at Jerusalem and in pointing there, they point to the One who will then be recognized by Israel as its Messiah. But how blessed we are to know Him already whom to know is life eternal. In that knowledge, our destiny lies. And what a destiny!—to see Him face to face . . . be like Him . . . have His name on our forehead . . . and reign with Him forever!

Footnotes

1. Genesis 14:17-20; Hebrews 7:1-10
2. Genesis 22:1-14
3. II Samuel 5:6-12
4. I Chronicles 21:24–22:2
5. Luke 2:21-24
6. Luke 2:41-47
7. Luke 19:38; Mark 11:9,10
8. John 19:15; Luke 23:18
9. Psalm 22
10. Matthew 27:46
11. Matthew 28:5,6
12. Acts 2:1-4
13. Daniel 9:27; Ezekiel 40–42
14. II Thessalonians 2:4
15. Revelation 11:1,2
16. Daniel 9:27
17. Revelation 13:14,15
18. Luke 21:24
19. Zechariah 14:2
20. Zechariah 14:4; 13:1
21. Zechariah 12:10
22. Zechariah 13:6
23. Joel 3:17
24. Joel 3:20,21
25. Isaiah 65:18-20
26. Zechariah 2:4,5

CHAPTER 9

What Next?

What time is it on the clock of biblical prophecy? Well, it all depends on where the question comes from.

The world may be at the very threshold of irrevocable ruin—a ruin that will leave its cities in piles of tangled steel and concrete; its terrain so churned by geological disasters that all topographical charts and maps will be obsolete; its population decimated.

The clock of prophecy indicates that *Israel* is about to enter an era of paradox—of unprecedented prosperity and security, and of horrible disaster. Israel's covenant with the Antichrist will establish the security of the sovereign rights of Israel as a nation. The Jews will no longer have to live under the threat of Arab invasion. Through some means, unknown at present, they will secure the site in Jerusalem now occupied by the Mosque of Omar, and will rebuild their Temple[1] and reinstitute sacrificial worship there.[2] This cannot happen until they are able to identify from among their population the Levitical priesthood. When Titus destroyed Jerusalem in A.D. 70, all genealogical records of Israel were lost. A few years ago the Jewish and Christian communities were thrilled to hear of the discovery of the Dead Sea Scrolls. History could repeat itself with the discovery, in some cave, of an authentic copy of the ancient genealogical records.

Fortune will smile upon the nation of Israel during the first three and one half years of the Tribulation period. Then disaster will strike! Freedom of worship will be suspended. Sacrificial worship will be forbidden. Idolatry will be enforced under threat of death.

Years ago in Babylon the Jews learned their lesson, and learned it well. Never again would they be guilty of idolatry. They have bowed beneath the yoke of slavery and foreign occupation. But since the Babylonian captivity, no power on earth has been able to compel them to worship idols. Antiochus Epiphanes tried it and discovered that even wholesale slaughter could not make the Jews an idolatrous people.

The Antichrist will make the same discovery and in the fury of his frustration he will bring to the nation of Israel the darkest day of its mostly dark history.

What is next for *the Church?* First, what do you mean by the term "Church"? If you are thinking of the nominal Christian communities—the councils and denominations—then nothing very different will immediately happen.

The ecumenical trend will continue to accelerate until the dream of church statesmen will become a reality. Probably this will not happen until after the Second Appearing of Christ and the removal of the Church, the Body of Christ and the Holy Spirit from this world.[3] Then the super church—the One World, One Faith monstrosity, called by John the "Great Whore," will dominate the religious life of the whole world and will be supported in its ambitions by the Beast.[4]

But the true Church, the living organism called in the Bible, the body of Christ,[5] is about to pass into its greatest moment and what a moment that will be! We are not only *looking* for signs, we are also *listening* for sounds—the shout of our precious Lord Jesus Christ as He descends from heaven to receive us unto Himself. No longer will we need an advocate for we shall be like Him.

He also has been waiting a long time for this moment and His shout of joy is understandable. The archangel's voice will extend heaven's welcome. The trumpet section of heaven's orchestra will herald this glorious event—the culmination of plans and announcements and prophecies through the ages.

But prophecy includes a post-rapture event for Christ's Church—the Judgment Seat of Christ.

Peter wrote, ". . . judgment must begin at the

house of God: and if it first begin at us, what shall the end be of them that obey not the gospel of God? And if the righteous scarcely be saved, where shall the ungodly and the sinner appear?"[6]

It was Paul who informed us that ". . . we shall all stand before the judgment seat of Christ. For it is written, As I live, saith the Lord, every knee shall bow to me, and every tongue shall confess to God. So then every one of us shall give account of himself to God."[7]

As though to emphasize the solemn importance of this prophetic announcement, Paul repeated it, "For we must all appear before the judgment seat of Christ; that every one may receive the things done in his body, according to that he hath done, whether it be good or bad."[8]

Further light is thrown upon this prophecy in another of Paul's letters where he writes, "Every man's work shall be made manifest: for the day shall declare it, because it shall be revealed by fire; and the fire shall try every man's work of what sort it is. If any man's work abide which he hath built thereupon, he shall receive a reward. If any man's work shall be burned, he shall suffer loss: but he himself shall be saved; yet so as by fire."[9]

This calls for some sober reflection. Someone has said, "It won't be all fun at the coming of Christ."

We know that our eternal salvation is not dependent upon our efforts or merit. We are saved by grace through faith. But there is more to eternity than escaping hell. Some will be saved "as by fire." Peter expressed concern that his beloved children in the faith should have a better experience when they meet Christ. "Give diligence to make your calling and election sure: for if ye do these things, ye shall never fall: for so an entrance shall be ministered unto you *abundantly* into the everlasting kingdom of our Lord and Saviour Jesus Christ."[10]

So the issue to be decided at the Judgment Seat of Christ is not one of our eternal destiny but rather concerning our faithfulness, or lack of it, as servants of Christ. As stewards of God, what have we done with our body which He gave us to use only to His glory? What use have we made of our time, our possessions, our abilities? What about the quality of our motives? To what extent have we fulfilled *His* plan for our lives? What have we done concerning the Great Commission?[11] Or have we relegated this responsibility to professional missionaries and pastors? What about our tithes? Will our lives and our works stand the "fire" test?

Some years ago a crack express train pulled into the Lehigh Valley railroad terminal in Jersey City, New Jersey. The engineer climbed down from his cab and with a rag and an oil can began his labor of love on his beloved iron monster. An elderly, well dressed passenger approached him, patted his shoulder and said, "Good run, sir. A good run." As the elderly gentleman walked away the fireman ran up to the engineer and demanded, "What did he say, John?" Nonchalantly the engineer replied, "Oh, he just said it was a good run. Why do you ask?"

"Why do I ask? Don't you know who that was? That was the president of our line!"

And may God so fill us with His love and guide us by His Spirit, that when we stand before the

Judgment Seat of Christ we may hear Him say, "That was a good run. Well done, thou good and faithful servant. Enter thou into the joy of thy Lord."[12]

Footnotes

1. Ezekiel 40–43
2. Ezekiel 43:19; Numbers 18:6
3. II Thessalonians 2:7; I Thessalonians 4:17
4. Revelation 17:1-6
5. I Corinthians 12:27; Colossians 1:18
6. I Peter 4:17,18
7. Romans 14:10-12
8. II Corinthians 5:10
9. I Corinthians 3:13-15
10. II Peter 1:10,11
11. Matthew 28:18-20
12. Matthew 25:21

CHAPTER 10

What's Holding Things Back?

There is no doubt about it. The world is going from bad to worse. More crime, more violence, more drugs, more smog, more divorces, higher taxes, more inflation—more of everything wrong and dangerous. And yet, it could be worse. It will be! But not yet.

Something is holding back the devil and all his organized forces of evil. As bad as they are, things are still under some measure of control.

Something, or someone greater than the law and the police forces, is keeping crime and lawlessness and violence from going off with a big bang.

According to statistics and trends the "big bang" should have come some yesterdays ago or it will come soon on one of these tomorrows. But it hasn't happened! Why?

The Bible gives the answer. We have seen it several times in this book. It is coined in strange language but it is there.

"Let no man deceive you by any means: for *that day shall not come,* except there come a falling away first, and that man of sin be revealed, the son of perdition; who opposeth and exalteth himself above all that is called God, or that is worshipped; so that he as God sitteth in the temple of God, shewing himself that he is God. Remember ye not, that, when I was yet with you, I told you these things? And now ye know what withholdeth [that which restrains] that he might be revealed in his time. For the mystery of iniquity doth already work; only he who now letteth [hindreth] will let [hinder], until he be taken out of the way. And then shall that Wicked be revealed . . ."[1]

To whom was Paul referring when he wrote, "he who now letteth [hindereth]"? There can be only one answer—the Holy Spirit. Who else would have the authority and power to hold back the sinister forces of the Antichrist?

So it is the Holy Spirit who is putting His foot on the brake and keeping this crazy old world from going over the cliff before its course is run. Presently He is in the driver's seat and He has two assistants—the Word of God and the Church. Wherever these three operate, the forces of evil are held in check. The greater the place given to them, the greater their restraining influence. As the Bible is evicted from our schools and discarded by our churches, and as the Holy Spirit is relegated to a secondary position in the lives and ministries of Christians, the forces of evil come creeping out of their dark holes and openly damn the souls of men. Missionaries who work on the front lines of evangelism have testified repeatedly to open demonstrations of demoniacal powers in opposition to the Gospel.

Many years ago, a man sitting in a barber shop was relating a filthy story. The door opened and in walked a portly gentleman. The moment he entered, the man who was telling the story stopped speaking as though a hand had been clapped over his mouth. After the gentleman had left, the storyteller turned to the barber and asked, "Who was that fellow, anyway? The funniest thing happened. The moment he walked in I completely forgot the rest of that story I was telling you." The barber replied, "That was the famous evangelist, Dwight L. Moody."

Yes, the Word of God and true Christians do have a restraining force over the powers of darkness. But at the second coming of Christ, every true child of God will be removed. That restraining power will be gone. Also, there is reason to believe that there may be a mysterious disappearance of the Word of God after the Church has been taken away.

Listen to this prophecy. "Behold, the days come, saith the Lord God, that I will send a famine in the land, not a famine of bread, nor a thirst for water, but of hearing the words of the Lord: and they shall wander from sea to sea, and from the north even to the east, they shall run to and fro to seek the word of the Lord, and shall not find it."[2] It is not difficult to believe that all copies of the Bible will be destroyed by the super church or the Antichrist, and the Word of God will be eliminated from this world.

Then, of course, the Holy Spirit as an abiding Person, will accompany the Church when she is caught away to be with Christ. The Spirit's relation to the world will return to that which existed in the days prior to Pentecost.

So every true Christian will be gone, the Word of God may disappear and the Holy Spirit will leave. So what? The answer staggers the imagination. If it is no longer safe for churches in the larger cities to hold evening services, if police units must patrol high school corridors, if atomic war clouds are blotting out all sunlight of hope for peace, if human life has no value whatever to organized crime—what will this world be like when all the reins have been cut and all restraining influences taken away?

I have seven precious grandchildren. I would rather see them die and bury them with my own hands than have them live on an earth that has gone completely mad with unbridled passions—where all anchors have been discarded—where there is no law and no decency. And then follow the unbelievable horrors and agony of the Great Tribulation judgments. And this will be the world of the end times.

Yes, the Holy Spirit is directly involved in prophecy. Not only does He prevent the premature unveiling of the Beast, He is engaged also in preparing the bride, the Church, for the coming of the Bridegroom. He convicts her when she goes astray and leads her back into fellowship with Christ.

He guides her into all truth, reveals the precious things of Christ to her and shows her things present and things to come.[3] When she gets defiled, He leads her to forgiveness and cleansing,[4] and reminds her that " . . . every man that hath this hope in him purifieth himself, even as he is pure."[5]

The Holy Spirit is also completing the Bride of Christ. In the Old Testament there is a beautiful story of Abraham sending his trusted senior servant Eliezer to secure a bride for his son Isaac.[6] In answer to prayer the servant found beautiful Rebekah, the daughter of Bethuel. When asked if she were willing to leave her family and home to travel far away to be the bride of Isaac, she simply said, "I will go."

About 1900 years ago the Father sent the Holy Spirit to this world to secure a bride for His Son. Even yet, in every country and culture, He is still seeking the completion of that bride. Each person who is led to receive the Lord Jesus Christ becomes a member of that bride. Soon, very soon, the bride will be complete and the Spirit will take her to meet her Bridegroom. And how does she feel about it? Like the Rebekah of long ago, she says, "I will go. Even so, come, Lord Jesus."

Footnotes

1. II Thessalonians 2:3-8
2. Amos 8:11,12
3. John 14:26; 16:13,14
4. I John 1:9
5. I John 3:3
6. Genesis 24

CHAPTER 11

Into the Night

The Second Appearing of Jesus Christ will usher in a new era for this world. It will be an age of new freedoms. No longer will there be evangelical missionaries and preachers to warn of judgment to come. The staffs of the great Christian movements will have disappeared. Unbelieving husbands will no longer be irritated by the pleas and prayers of wives and children to receive Christ as Saviour. They too will be missing. Millions of people from all walks of life will have mysteriously and instantly ceased to exist on this earth. Drivers of cars, pilots of planes, school teachers—thousands of them will be here one moment and gone the next! But there will be one common denominator—all who will be missing will be those who "took their religion too seriously"—the fanatics.

The news media will have plenty to talk about but they will have no explanation for what has happened. Newspapers around the world will carry screaming headlines—MILLIONS MISSING! Husbands, bereft of wife and children, will go insane with grief. *They* will know what has happened. They will remember the warnings, the tearful pleading, the loving prayers which they ignored, or brushed off with a gruff, "Don't push me. There's plenty of time."

But it is probable that the disappearance of the Christians will bring a sense of relief to most people to whom their lives of purity, their standards of righteousness, their persistent witness of Christ had been a constant source of annoyance.

Within a short time, the church sanctuaries will become public buildings or recreation centers. The courts will be busy taking care of the many legal problems created by the abandonment of real estate and funds by the missing ones.

But the relief of the situation produced by Christ's Second Appearing will soon be forgotten in the terror that shall grip the world. Suddenly all law and order will be gone. Every man will do that which is right in his own eyes—the rest of the people and the world be damned! Families will break up because natural affection will no longer exist.[1] Governments and law enforcement agencies will crumble beneath the juggernaut of anarchy. All peace will be taken from the earth.[2] Every nation, city and family will be embroiled in conflict. The economy and industry of the world will collapse. Famine on a scale never previously known will become world-wide.[3] Suicides, wars, riots, famines, crime—all will take their grim toll until twenty-five percent of humanity has perished.[4] And then the "saviour" will appear—the Beast, the Antichrist, the real Super Man! Out of chaos, he will bring order. Out of anarchy, he will bring government. Out of famine, he will bring plenty. Out of depression he will bring prosperity. Soon the world will be groveling at his feet. And why not?

This amazing man will be able to present scientific proof that he had been dead for hundreds of years.[5]

He will demonstrate a supernatural ability to bring world-wide peace and restore economic prosperity.[6]

Together with his promotion agent, the False Prophet, he will baffle the world of science by performing amazing miracles.[7]

He will secure the endorsement of the World Church[8] and control of world finance, probably through his covenant with the Jews.[9]

The political situation will begin to jell and will finally culminate in the formation of an administrative government located at Rome, the "seven hills" city.[10] The major authority of this world government will center in ten nations quite similar in geographic coverage to the old Roman Empire.[11]

Yes, the Beast will have little difficulty in convincing the world that he is the real Super Man.

But that will not satisfy his evil ambitions. One morning the news media of the world will receive a news release from the Antichrist's palace in Rome. "WORLD EMPEROR REVEALS HIS TRUE IDENTITY!" Then will follow the startling announcement that the Super Man is actually the "Super God" and is prepared to prove it! The world is invited to attend, or to view on their television screens, an amazing demonstration of his divine powers in the Jewish Temple in Jerusalem.

The day arrives. Thousands of the top-level world leaders arrive in the crowded city. Angry Jewish priests and religious leaders are vainly attempting to prevent workmen from moving a giant metal statue of the Antichrist into the Temple sanctuary. The World Emperor arrives and, sensing the problem, confers for a moment with the False Prophet. Mounting the platform erected in the center of the Temple courtyard, he holds up his hands for silence. But the Jews are not to be so easily silenced. The High Priest approaches the platform, his face livid with anger. He cries, "You've lied to us. You are breaking our covenant. Take that blasphemous idol from these sacred portals!"

A smile of disdain appears on the face of the Antichrist. And then his voice rings out over the crowd, "As God, I cannot tolerate such insolence. Perish, you fool!"

Instantly there is a flash of blinding fire from the clear sky, striking the High Priest, enveloping him, and then disappearing as suddenly as it came! And where the High Priest had been standing, there is only a small mound of ashes with a wisp of smoke rising from it.[12] A deafening roar of amazement and approval rises from the thousands of spectators. "He *is* God! He *is* God!"

But the real demonstration is yet to come. The statue has been placed in the center of the main entrance to the Temple. It is a remarkable likeness. The midmorning sun gleams from its polished metal. A small but high platform is placed by its side. The False Prophet, known to the world as the Antichrist's Prime Minister, mounts the platform and addresses the crowd. "You have seen our Emperor God demonstrate his power in judgment upon this Jew. Now we will remove from your mind any lingering doubt that he is in truth what he claims to be, the only true God."

Then turning toward the statue, he places his hand upon the metal head, and says, "In the name and through the power of our great Emperor and the only true God, I command that you live and that you speak."

The silence is so intense it can almost be felt! And then it happens! The metal eyes open! A metal arm rises and points a finger toward the small mound of ashes. The lips separate, the mouth opens and in thundering tones the statue speaks, "So perish all those who do not worship the only true God, the Emperor."[13]

John recorded what follows, "And all the world wondered after the beast. And they worshipped the dragon [Satan] which gave power unto the beast: and they worshipped the beast, saying, Who is like unto the beast? who is able to make war with him? . . . And all that dwell upon the earth shall worship him, whose names are not written in the book of life of the Lamb slain from the foundation of the world."[14]

Now heaven reacts. Such blasphemy can no longer be ignored. The scroll of judgment is given into the hands of the Lamb slain from the foundation of the world.[15] All heaven erupts into jubilant praise and adulation.

"Thou art worthy to take the book, and to open the seals thereof: for thou wast slain, and hast redeemed us to God by thy blood out of every kindred, and tongue, and people, and nation; and hast made us unto our God kings and priests: and we shall reign on the earth. . . . Worthy is the Lamb that was slain to receive power, and riches, and wisdom, and strength, and honour, and glory, and blessing . . . Blessing, and honour, and glory, and power, be unto him that sitteth upon the throne, and unto the Lamb for ever and ever."[16]

The Lamb opens the scroll. One by one the seals are broken. Judgments, swift and terrible, follow: anarchy, murder, violence,[17] famine,[18] death,[19] the prayers of the martyrs for vengeance,[20] the terrifying revelation of the face of God and the Lamb.[21] And then even more frightening, "silence in heaven,"[22] for it shall usher in the seven trumpet judgments that shall shatter the kingdom of the Beast and bring such agony to his subjects that they will "seek death, and shall not find it; and shall desire to die, and death shall flee from them."[23]

The most tragic part of this prophetic story is the human reaction to God's warnings and judgments. "And the rest of the men which were not killed by these plagues yet repented not of the works of their hands, that they should not worship devils, and idols of gold, and silver, and brass, and stone, and of wood: which neither can see, nor hear, nor walk: neither repented they of their murders, nor of their sorceries, nor of their fornication, nor of their thefts."[24]

But this is God's day of wrath. There will be no surcease from judgment until the last fragment of human resistance has been destroyed and the vile Beast and his prophet have met their just deserts. Yet, amazingly, even in the midst of judgment, God continues to appeal for repentance.

Two men of mystery appear in Jerusalem. Who they are and where they come from no one knows. Standing before the living statue of the Beast they warn its worshipers of the terrible consequence of their idolatry. Day after day, rain or shine, their voices are raised in fearless exposure of the Man of Sin and condemnation of his blasphemy. The news media carry their message to all the world, and it activates the long dormant voice of conscience. The world never wants to be told it is wrong and evil, and especially the world of the Antichrist. Resentment against the two preachers grows and then develops into violent, murderous hatred.

Attempts are made upon the lives of the Two Witnesses. They fail. In fact, it becomes the most dangerous thing a man can do. "If any man will hurt them, fire proceedeth out of their mouth, and devoureth their enemies: and if any man will hurt them, he must in this manner be killed."[25]

To support their message, they perform other

miracles—"These have power to shut heaven, that it rain not in the days of their prophecy: and have power over waters to turn them to blood, and to smite the earth with all plagues, as often as they will."[26]

Do I take this literally? Of course I do; just as literally as I take the Exodus account of Moses turning the water of the Nile into blood.

Three and a half years have gone by since the Two Witnesses first made their appearance. What success do they have? Only eternity will reveal that. Strangely, during all this time, the Antichrist has made no attempt to silence them.

Then the day of reckoning arrives. How it shall happen and with what weapon we are not told. John merely tells us, "And when they shall have finished their testimony, the beast that ascendeth out of the bottomless pit shall make war against them, and shall overcome them, and kill them."[27]

What will be the world's reaction? Let's call it, "Hell's Christmas." "And their dead bodies shall lie in the street of the great city, which spiritually is called Sodom and Egypt, where also our Lord was crucified [Jerusalem]. And they of the people and kindreds and tongues and nations shall see their dead bodies three days and an half, and shall not suffer their dead bodies to be put in graves. And they that dwell upon the earth shall rejoice over them, and make merry, and shall send gifts one to another; because these two prophets tormented them that dwelt on the earth."[28]

TV networks will carry the view of their decaying corpses to the whole world. Charter flights will probably carry the 7,000 world leaders to Jerusalem to enjoy the spectacle. But this will not be the end of the story. Let John complete it.

"And after three days and an half the spirit of life from God entered into them, and they stood upon their feet; and great fear fell upon them which saw them. And they heard a great voice from heaven saying unto them, Come up hither. And they ascended up to heaven in a cloud; and their enemies beheld them. And the same hour was there a great earthquake, and the tenth part of the city fell, and in the earthquake were slain of men seven thousand [the great men]."[29]

Who are the Two Witnesses? Some students of prophecy believe they will be Moses and Elijah, basing this upon the appearance of these two men upon the Mount of Transfiguration. Others believe they will be Elijah and Enoch, the only two humans who have passed from earth without experiencing death. They support this interpretation by pointing to the statement of Scripture, "It is appointed unto men once to die . . ."[30] Still others take this entire prophecy symbolically.

The Two Witnesses have now gone, but God has not yet completed His acts of judgment upon the kingdom of the Beast. In heaven there is heard "a great voice out of the temple saying to the seven angels, Go your ways, and pour out the vials [bowls] of the wrath of God upon the earth."[31] Now the Beast and his subjects will find that, "It is a fearful thing to fall into the hands of the living God."[32] The world has been moving into its night, but the darkest hours are still ahead.

The bowls of wrath are poured out "upon the men which had the mark of the beast, and upon them which worshipped his image."[33] Hideous ulcers, incurable and unbearably painful . . . drinking water turned into blood . . . sunburn of a severity never before known . . . darkness that could be felt and caused men to gnaw their tongues for pain—electrical storms and an earthquake of unprecedented severity—the greatest in human history, destroying every city in the world, leveling the mountains and submerging islands under the seas. And then to add to the horror and carnage, hailstones weighing about one hundred pounds fall from the skies, crushing and destroying anything standing after the earthquake.[34]

Can puny man still raise his fist of rebellion against an angry God? Incredibly, he does! Looking through the eyes of prophecy upon that shattered earth, John tells us, "And men were scorched with great heat, and blasphemed the name of God, which hath power over these plagues: and they repented not to give him glory . . . And blasphemed the God of heaven because of their pains and their sores, and repented not of their deeds . . . and men blasphemed God because of the plague of hail; for the plague thereof was exceeding great."[35]

Rome Has Fallen! The world capital of sin and sensuality is wiped out of existence by a stroke of divine judgment![36] And so fearful is its destruction that for miles around the land is considered unsafe.[37] The world mourns but heaven rejoices.[38]

In his insane rage, the Antichrist concludes that the Jews are responsible for all his misfortune. The armies of the world are mustered and now the Jews face the darkest hour of *their* night.

Looking down the corridors of time, the prophet Zechariah tells us what will happen. "Behold, the day of the Lord cometh, and thy spoil shall be divided in the midst of thee. For I will gather all nations against Jerusalem to battle; and the city shall be taken, and the houses rifled, and the women ravished; and half of the city shall go forth into captivity, and the residue of the people shall not be cut off from the city. . . ."[39]

"Behold, I will make Jerusalem a cup of trembling unto all the people round about, when they shall be in the siege both against Judah and against Jerusalem. And in that day will I make Jerusalem a burdensome stone for all people: all that burden themselves with it shall be cut in pieces, though all the people of the earth be gathered together against it."[40]

The prophet Joel adds his description of this day of Israel's trouble. "I will also gather all nations, and will bring them down into the valley of Jehoshaphat, and will plead with them there for my people and for my heritage Israel, whom they have scattered among the nations, and parted my land. And they have cast lots for my people; and have given a boy for an harlot, and sold a girl for wine, that they might drink . . . ye have taken my silver and my gold, and have carried into your temples my goodly pleasant things: the children also of Judah and the children of Jerusalem have ye sold unto the Grecians, that ye might remove them far from their border."[41]

So fierce will be the savagery of the Beast and his armies that when the dust of battle finally lifts from the land of Israel, only one third of its inhabitants will have survived. "And it shall come to pass, that in all the land, saith the Lord, two parts therein shall be cut off and die; but the third shall be left therein."[42]

The forces of the Antichrist will withdraw from the doomed city to celebrate their victory and make preparations to go back and finish the job. There will be no hope for Israel and the people will know it. They have only one way to look–up to God. Will they finally do it?

Footnotes

1. II Timothy 3:3
2. Revelation 6:4
3. Revelation 6:5,6
4. Revelation 6:8
5. Revelation 13:3,4; 17:8
6. Revelation 13:7; Daniel 8:24,25
7. Revelation 13:13,14
8. Revelation 17:1-8
9. Daniel 9:27;11:43
10. Revelation 17:9,18
11. Revelation 17:12; Daniel 2:40-43
12. Revelation 13:13
13. Revelation 13:15
14. Revelation 13:3,4,8
15. Revelation 5:6-14
16. Revelation 5:9,10,12,13

17. Revelation 6:3,4
18. Revelation 6:5,6
19. Revelation 6:8
20. Revelation 6:9,10
21. Revelation 6:12-17
22. Revelation 8:1
23. Revelation 9:6
24. Revelation 9:20,21
25. Revelation 11:3-5
26. Revelation 11:6
27. Revelation 11:7
28. Revelation 11:8-10
29. Revelation 11:11-13
30. Hebrews 9:27
31. Revelation 16:1
32. Hebrews 10:31
33. Revelation 16:2
34. Revelation 16:3-21
35. Revelation 16:9,11,21
36. Revelation 18
37. Revelation 18:17
38. Revelation 18:9-20
39. Zechariah 14:1,2
40. Zechariah 12:2,3
41. Joel 3:2,3,5,6
42. Zechariah 13:8

CHAPTER 12

Prophecy, U.S.A.

Where does the United States fit into biblical prophecy, or doesn't it? Is it likely that God would not include in His plan of the ages a nation with such a noble origin and which under His blessing has grown to such a position of international power and influence? Or did America, like Topsy of *Uncle Tom's Cabin,* "just grow?"

Remember that in the Bible, Gentile nations are dealt with to the extent of their relation to and influence upon Israel. So the real question is, does the United States of America have any bearing upon Israel in its history, in its contemporary life or in its future? The answer is yes to all three issues.

Since its birth, the United States has always been a harbor for the refugee Jews. They had a part in its conception and in its independence. By the scores of thousands they have fled from Spain, Germany, Russia and other countries for refuge from persecution. True, there have been sporadic incidents of anti-Semitism but these have never reflected the national attitude.

After England's shameful breach of honesty with the Zionists, they never would have been able to secure and defend a national homeland but for the political and financial support of American citizens, many of Jewish origin.

Presently, the United States is pouring vast sums of money—millions of dollars in tourism alone and in essential military hardware—to assist the valiant little nation of Israel. It is possible that its only hope for survival is continued American friendship and assistance.

History proves that God has never failed to reward a nation which has extended a helping hand to the Jews. Is it not possible that much of our national prosperity may be attributed to this fact?

But what about the future? Will the United States play a future part in the fulfillment of biblical prophecy?

There are two possibilities, and we present them *only* as possibilities, for it is impossible to definitely identify any Bible references with the United States.

Israel will need a place of refuge when she is persecuted by the Beast, during the last half of the Great Tribulation. "And the woman [Israel] fled into the wilderness, where she hath a place prepared of God, that they should feed her there a thousand two hundred and threescore days [three and a half years]."[1] Could the United States be the place "prepared by God" as a refuge for the Jews? It was once a wilderness and certainly God has played a part in its prosperity and growth.

Years ago, some popular teachers of prophecy predicted that Petra, the ancient impregnable stronghold of the Edomites, would be the place where Israel would find refuge during the Great Tribulation. In fact, some of these teachers raised funds to place in Petra copies of the Scriptures, especially those Scriptures having to do with the future of Israel. It seemed like a good idea *then,* but with the development of modern weapons of war, Petra would provide no more protection for Israel today than would an open field.

So there is this possibility that the United States has been blessed and prepared by God as a refuge for His people from the wrath of Satan and the Beast.[2] But there is another possibility, and Ezekiel brings it to our attention.[3]

The prophet in dramatic fashion writes of a coming attack upon Israel by Russia: "Son of man, set thy face against Gog [the ruler or prince], the land of Magog [his land, Russia], the chief prince of Meshech [Moscow] and Tubal [Tobolsk], and prophesy against him . . . in the latter years thou shalt come into the land that is brought back from the sword, and is gathered out of many people, against the mountains of Israel, which have been always waste: but it is brought forth out of the nations, and they shall dwell safely all of them. Thou shalt ascend and come like a storm, thou shalt be like a cloud to cover the land, thou and all thy bands, and many people with thee."[4]

Among students of biblical prophecy there is unusual unanimity concerning the interpretation of this passage. Nearly all of them agree that this predicts an attack on the land of Israel by the military forces of Russia. But there is much disagreement concerning *when* this attack will be launched. Some say it will happen as part of the battle of Armageddon. Others put it a thousand years later, at the close of the Millennium.

All prophecy related to the battle of Armageddon indicates a *united* attack upon Israel and *upon the Lamb of God.* There is no indication of an independent attack by any one nation. Further, the motive of the Antichrist is not to get spoil, for he will have gotten that in his previous attack upon the land of Israel, but rather to defeat Christ and maintain his claim of deity. On the other hand, Ezekiel makes it very clear that Russia's purpose in launching its attack will be to despoil the countries it attacks.[5]

The possibility that Ezekiel's prophecy refers to the post-Millennial period is not probable. When Satan is loosed for a short season, following the Millennium, he will energize an attack by Gog and Magog, and other nations. John writes of that incident, "And they went up on the breadth of the earth, and compassed the camp of the saints about, and the beloved city: and fire came down from God out of heaven, and devoured [incinerated] them."[6]

Going back to Ezekiel's account of Russia's attack upon Israel, we find that following the destruction of five-sixths of the Russian forces,[7] the entire nation of Israel will be conscripted *to bury* the dead Russians. And it will take them seven months to do so.[8] This will be mass burial, not mass cremation.

A careful study of the reign and the character of the Beast indicates that he will tolerate no competition or failure to cooperate. Also indicated is the fact that his control and political influence will be international and supreme. Even more significant, his ideology will not be atheistic but homo-deistic. He will place a great emphasis upon religion. Worship will be compulsory. So it would seem unlikely that the Antichrist and the communist ideology could coexist. So there remains the possibility that Russia's wide influence will be shattered by a catastrophic divine judgment upon her as she is in the process of attacking Israel. This would leave the field open for the Beast to establish his empire.

None of this brings the United States into the prophetic picture. But Ezekiel has more to say.

"Thus saith the Lord God; It shall also [in addition to the previous plan to attack Israel] come to pass, that at the same time shall things come into thy mind, and thou shalt think an evil thought: and thou shalt say, I will go up to the land of unwalled villages [open country]; I will go to them that are at rest, that dwell safely, all of them dwelling without walls [fortifications], and having neither bars nor gates, to take a spoil, and to take a prey; to turn thine hand upon the desolate places that are now inhabited, and upon the people that are gathered out of the nations, which have gotten cattle and goods, that dwell in the midst of the land.'"[9]

It would be difficult to find a better word picture of the United States, and at the same time it is *not* a proper description of Israel. From coast to coast, and from Mexico to Canada there are no fortifications. We are a nation of unwalled cities, dwelling without fortifications.

Prior to the establishing of the American colonies, the land was and always had been without cities or civilization—"the desolate places."

No other nation has ever been called, "The Melting Pot." They came to us by the millions from Europe, Asia, Africa and the Orient. "The people that are gathered out of the nations" followed the glow of the torch of liberty to its source. They heard and responded to the invitation,

"Give me your tired, your poor,
Your huddled masses yearning to be free,
The wretched refuse of your teeming shore.
Send these, the homeless, tempest-tost to me.
I lift my lamp beside the golden door."

—Emma Lazarus.

And in coming, most of them found a standard of living that exceeded their fondest dreams. They became a people that "have gotten cattle and goods." Never have so many people had so much—the richest nation in the world, and therein lies its greatest danger. It has become the object of envy to leaders of other nations who have craved more territory and more power and more wealth.

Ezekiel wrote of those ". . . that dwell in the midst of the land." Yes, we in the United States dwell "from sea to shiny sea." We see the morning sun rise over our Atlantic and watch it set in golden splendor over our Pacific.

One of the unusual features of life in America is the emphasis placed upon leisure. Vacations, sports, hobbies, coffee breaks, tours, picnics, hikes—the list is endless. Eight-hour work days are yielding to six-hour days, and within a short time few Americans will be working more than four days a week. Ezekiel prophesied that Russia will say, "I will go to them that are at rest [ease]."[10]

Few of these characteristics of American life could be applied to Israel. From border to border, it is an armed camp. It is not a wealthy nation. Its essential military budget keeps it tottering on the tightrope of economic disaster. They are not at rest. Few people in the world work as hard and as willingly as do the people of Israel.

We are therefore suggesting the possibility that according to Ezekiel's prophesy, Russia will attack not only Israel but the United States as well. But Russia's defeat will not come through force of arms but through divine intervention.

These two prophetic possibilities are closely related. *If* the United States is to be the place of refuge for the Jews, then our nation stands in need of a spiritual housecleaning. Nationally we have forgotten God. Since there is no indication that we will of our own volition "humble [ourselves], and pray, and seek [God's] face, and turn from [our] wicked ways,"[11] it may be necessary for God to accomplish the same thing through a Russian military attack upon our nation.

"And when these things begin to come to pass, then look up, and lift up your heads; for your redemption draweth nigh."[12]

Footnotes

1. Revelation 12:6
2. Revelation 12:13-16
3. Ezekiel 38,39
4. Ezekiel 38:2-9
5. Ezekiel 38:13
6. Revelation 20:7-9
7. Ezekiel 39:2
8. Ezekiel 39:11-15
9. Ezekiel 38:10-12
10. Ezekiel 38:11
11. II Chronicles 7:14
12. Luke 21:28

CHAPTER 13

The Mark of the Beast

Few Americans realized the full significance of what occurred on June 16, 1933, when the NRA (National Recovery Act) became part of the governmental machinery of the United States.

The Depression had taken its bitter toll. Economic, industrial and financial collapse left the nation in a position quite similar to what the world will experience in the first few months of the Great Tribulation. Hunger, unemployment, panic, suicides—all became the daily pattern of national life.

The NRA gave the federal government control over the major industries of the country. Business men were required to open their books to government inspection. A federal "Blue Eagle" was stamped on products by the producers submitting to the codes. Violators of the blanket code imposed by the President had their "Blue Eagle" taken away from them and this forced many of them out of business.

While people went hungry, thousands of hogs were slaughtered, their meat poisoned and buried. Mountains of grains and farm produce were destroyed in order to raise prices. Citizens of "the land of the free, and the home of the brave" meekly submitted to a presidential edict which made it practically impossible to buy or sell anything that was not stamped with NRA's "Blue Eagle."

Many Bible students then, and now, have wondered if this was not a dress rehearsal for the Antichrist's "Mark of the Beast." What is the "Mark of the Beast"?

When Christ makes His Second Appearing to snatch from this world His church, the Antichrist will soon reveal himself to the world.

Endowed by Satan with supernatural power and authority, he will be able to bring calm out of panic, prosperity out of depression and peace out of anarchy. The people of the world will be so grateful that they will without hesitation or question submit to any action he will take.

The Antichrist will establish an efficient and stable government similar to and covering approximately the same areas as Imperial Rome. His word will become law.

Through miracles, called by the apostle Paul "lying wonders,"[1] he will win the admiration and allegiance of men. In time, all the world will wonder after this amazing Super Man. Who is he? Where did he come from? Where does he get his power? Is he man or is he God? The world will ask these questions and the Antichrist will answer them.

The Bible does not give us his name, but narrows the choice to seven historical kings. We do know that the world will be impressed by the fact that the Antichrist had a deadly wound and yet was able to live. He may be able to prove that he came from the dead.

We also know that the Antichrist will not hesitate to reveal to men the source of his power and authority—the Dragon (Satan)—and he will lead humanity into devil worship.[2] This will not be difficult. Even now the world is moving rapidly in that direction.

Worship of Satan is being practiced openly both in this country and in Europe. Edifices of worship dedicated to the devil have been erected. Witchcraft is being taught in a western university. Leading churchmen have made no apology for being involved in spiritism. More and more psychiatrists are admitting the existence and activities of strange demonic forces. One of the world's greatest newspapers accidentally omitted from one issue its usual column of astrology. Its switchboard was jammed with more frantic calls and complaints than it had ever received in its history.

As his influence spreads, the Antichrist will tighten his grip on the reins of politics, industry and economics. And then it will occur!

One morning, during the Great Tribulation, the

world citizens will awaken to the news that its wonder man, the Antichrist, has decided that new regulations are necessary to avoid an economic recession. Actually, it will be a radical move toward religious totalitarianism.

The world government will make available immediately to all public relations offices the equipment necessary for stamping an official insignia upon every citizen of the world government. The Antichrist will decide that in the future no one may buy or sell any product or conduct any business unless he has the "Mark of the Beast" indelibly stamped upon his forehead or on the palm of his right hand.[3] The Bible does not tell us what that mark will be, except to say it will identify the wearer with the Antichrist. It will be *his* mark.[4]

Some students of the Bible believe the "Mark of the Beast" will be the number "666" because of John's statement, "He that had . . . the name of the beast, or the number of his name . . . and his number is Six hundred threescore and six."[5]

Whatever the hellish mark will be, it will identify its possessor as an endorser of the Antichrist's policies and as one of his worshipers.

Will the people of the world ever submit to this indignity? Our proud Americans submitted to the mark of the NRA's "Blue Eagle" without a national protest in 1933! And the people of the Antichrist's world will probably vie with each other in seeing who will be the first to receive that vile brand.

Suppose some will refuse to be branded? Many people will. What will happen to them? It does not take much imagination to answer that question.

What would happen to you if from this moment you could not buy or sell *anything* or conduct *any* business whatever? No food, clothing, utilities, transportation, gasoline, banking, education, medication—nothing!

Children will cry for food that cannot be bought. Families will be evicted from homes because rent and mortgage payments will not be accepted. Automobiles will rust in garages because oil companies will not sell gas to anyone without the "Mark." Water, light and gas will be turned off because your money or check will not be honored. Life will become grim and then impossible for those who refuse to be branded by Satan's Antichrist. Death will stalk these victims of righteousness.

But there will be another news release issued by the world government. Even more inhuman regulations will be announced. Newspaper headlines will break the news, "BE BRANDED OR DIE." Special police will roam the streets looking for unmarked rebels. In the middle of the night, doors will be battered open by secret agents and flashlights will be focused on the foreheads and right hands of the startled occupants. Without trial or mercy or respect for sex or age, all those discovered without the "Mark" will be executed.

During his reign of terror, the Antichrist will reinstitute two ancient practices—slavery[6] and execution by decapitation.[7] Blood will flow freely as many brave souls who have found God through the faithful witness of His messengers[8] will lay down their lives "for the word of God, and for the testimony which they held."[9]

When the kingdom of the Antichrist comes to a catastrophic end at Armageddon it will be the blasphemous "Mark of the Beast" that will become the mark of doom for its wearers, ". . . them that had received the mark of the beast . . . were slain with the sword of him that sat upon the horse, which sword proceeded out of his mouth: and all the fowls were filled with their flesh."[10]

Do I surprise you when I say that I hope to be branded some day—not with the "Mark of the Beast," but with another mark? John tells us about it.

"And there shall be no more curse: but the throne of God and of the Lamb shall be in it [The New Jerusalem]; and his servants shall serve him: and they shall see his face; and HIS NAME SHALL BE IN THEIR FOREHEADS."[11]

"O That Will Be Glory For Me."

Footnotes

1. II Thessalonians 2:9
2. Revelation 13:4
3. Revelation 13:16
4. Revelation 13:17
5. Revelation 13:17,18
6. Zechariah 14:2; Joel 3:3
7. Revelation 20:4
8. Revelation 11:3-12
9. Revelation 6:9
10. Revelation 19:20,21
11. Revelation 22:3,4

CHAPTER 14

Blood to Swim In!

For many centuries God has been pleading with Israel to look up to Jehovah—to turn from its perversity and unbelief, but all in vain. In tender love God's call went out, "Hear, O heavens, and give ear, O earth; for the Lord hath spoken, I have nourished and brought up children, and they have rebelled against me. The ox knoweth his owner, and the ass his master's crib: but Israel doth not know, my people doth not consider. Ah sinful nation, a people laden with iniquity, a seed of evildoers, children that are corrupters: they have forsaken the Lord, they have provoked the Holy One of Israel unto anger, they are gone away backward . . . Your country is desolate, your cities are burned with fire: your land, strangers devour it in your presence, and it is desolate, as overthrown by strangers . . . Except the Lord of hosts had left unto us a very small remnant, we should have been as Sodom, and we should have been like unto Gomorrah."[1]

This will be the condition Israel will find itself in after the invasion of the Beast. Over the gates of Jerusalem a placard might be placed, "ABANDON ALL HOPE WHO ENTER HERE."

And then it will happen! Someone, a priest or one of the godly remnant, will proclaim the message of Joel: "Therefore also now, saith the Lord, turn ye even to me with all your heart, and with fasting, and with weeping, and with mourning: and rend your heart, and not your garments, and turn unto the Lord your God: for he is gracious and merciful, slow to anger, and of great kindness, and repenteth him of the evil . . . Let the priests, the ministers of the Lord, weep between the porch and the altar, and let them say, Spare thy people, O Lord, and give not thine heritage to reproach, that the heathen should rule over them: wherefore should they say among the people, Where is their God?"[2]

And for the first time in all their checkered history, the people of Israel will turn *with all their hearts* unto the Lord their God.

"And I will pour upon the house of David, and upon the inhabitants of Jerusalem, the spirit of grace and of supplications: and they shall look upon me whom they have pierced, and they shall mourn for him, as one mourneth for his only son . . . In that day shall there be a great mourning in Jerusalem

. . . And the land shall mourn, every family apart."[3]

And God will hear and answer. "In that day there shall be a fountain opened to the house of David and to the inhabitants of Jerusalem for sin and for uncleanness."[4]

And what a revival it will be! A nation will be reborn in a day—into fellowship with God. "And it shall come to pass afterward, that I will pour out my spirit upon all flesh; and your sons and your daughters shall prophesy, your old men shall dream dreams, your young men shall see visions: And also upon the servants and upon the handmaids in those days will I pour out my spirit . . . And it shall come to pass, that whosoever shall call on the name of the Lord shall be delivered."[5]

It will be Pentecost all over again. "For then will I turn to the people a pure language, that they may all call upon the name of the Lord, to serve him with one consent."[6]

While the Spirit of God will be working within Jerusalem, Satan will be preparing the Beast and his armies without the city for the final attack that will forever make the words "Jew" and "Israel" obsolete terms.

"Then shall the Lord go forth, and fight against those nations, as when he fought in the day of battle."[7]

The prophet Joel dramatically describes what will happen. "I will also gather all nations, and will bring them down into the valley of Jehoshaphat, and will plead with them there for my people . . . Proclaim ye this among the Gentiles; Prepare war, wake up the mighty men, let all the men of war draw near; let them come up: Beat your plowshares into swords, and your pruninghooks into spears: let the weak say, I am strong.

"Assemble yourselves, and come, all ye heathen, and gather yourselves together round about: thither cause thy mighty ones to come down, O Lord. Let the heathen be wakened, and come up to the valley of Jehoshaphat: for there will I sit to judge all the heathen round about. Put ye in the sickle, for the harvest is ripe: come, get you down; for the press is full, the fats overflow; for their wickedness is great.

"Multitudes, multitudes in the valley of decision: for the day of the Lord is near in the valley of decision. The sun and the moon shall be darkened, and the stars shall withdraw their shining. The Lord also shall roar out of Zion, and utter his voice from Jerusalem; and the heavens and the earth shall shake: but the Lord will be the hope of his people, and the strength of the children of Israel."[8]

Where will the Church be when all these things will be occurring? What will happen to the saints after they appear before the Judgment Seat of Christ?[9]

There will be a wedding! Christ, the Bridegroom, and the Church, the bride,[10] will be joined in eternal union at heavenly festivities.[11] Then the saints will become actual "joint-heirs with Christ," and "so shall we ever be with the Lord."[12]

When Christ faces and defeats the Antichrist, we will participate in His victory. When He reigns as King of kings and Lord of lords we shall reign with Him.[13]

Therefore, when Jesus comes the second time to

this earth in power and great glory, we shall come with Him.[14] We will stand by His side on the Mount of Olives.

The apostle Paul prophesied of the same event, "The Lord Jesus shall be revealed from heaven with his mighty angels, in flaming fire taking vengeance on them that know not God, and that obey not the gospel of our Lord Jesus Christ: who shall be punished with everlasting destruction from the presence of the Lord, and from the glory of his power."[15]

Describing His Second Coming, Jesus said, "The sun shall be darkened, and the moon shall not give her light, and the stars shall fall from heaven, and the powers of the heavens shall be shaken: And then shall appear the sign of the Son of man in heaven: and then shall all the tribes of the earth mourn, and they shall see the Son of man coming in the clouds of heaven with power and great glory."[16]

"And his feet shall stand in that day upon the mount of Olives, which is before Jerusalem on the east."[17]

The stage is all set. All the actors are in their positions. Israel has truly repented. In answer to their cry to God, Jesus Christ has come and revealed Himself to the Jews. They see the nail holes in His hands and weep over them. The armies of the world gather in the valley of Megiddo. The Mount of Olives has been split into two hills by a mighty earthquake that occurred when the feet of Jesus touched it.[17]

An angel stands in the sun and calls for the birds

and beasts of prey to assemble for God's great banquet.[18]

The Beast and his armies decide to take the initiative and launch an attack upon Jesus Christ.[19] Blinded by Satan, they rush forward against the Son of God. What fools! Don't they realize—can't they see they have no chance even for survival?

With his prophetic vision, the apostle John saw what the odds were. "And I saw heaven opened, and behold a white horse: and he that sat upon him was called Faithful and True, and in righteousness he doth judge and make war.

"His eyes were as a flame of fire, and on his head were many crowns; and he had a name written, that no man knew, but he himself. And he was clothed with a vesture dipped in blood: and his name is called The Word of God.

"And the armies which were in heaven followed him upon white horses, clothed in fine linen, white and clean.

"And out of his mouth goeth a sharp sword, that with it he should smite the nations: and he shall rule them with a rod of iron: and he treadeth the winepress of the fierceness and wrath of Almighty God.

"And he hath on his vesture and on his thigh a name written, KING OF KINGS, AND LORD OF LORDS."[20]

The Bible likens the ensuing carnage to the treading of a winepress. "And the angel thrust in his sickle into the earth, and gathered the vine of the earth, and cast it into the great winepress of the wrath of God.

"And the winepress was trodden without the city, and BLOOD CAME OUT OF THE WINEPRESS, EVEN UNTO THE HORSE BRIDLES, BY THE SPACE OF A THOUSAND AND SIX HUNDRED FURLONGS."[21]

A river of blood—two hundred miles long and five feet deep! Blood to swim in!

The men of the world had for ages past shed the blood of saints and prophets.[22] They had clamored for and gloated over the blood of God's two witnesses, slain by the Beast.[23] They had joined in the murderous assault upon the Jews. Now their blood is added to the vintage of God's winepress of wrath. They have discovered, when it was too late, that "the wages of sin is death."[24] They could have been saved from the wrath of God by the application of the sin-cleansing blood of Christ. But they trampled upon that precious blood, and now their corpses float in a river of blood!

The blood of Christ when believed and received, *saves*. The blood of Christ when rejected, *damns*, for it becomes evidence of rebellion against God.

Footnotes

1. Isaiah 1:2-4,7,9
2. Joel 2:12,13,17
3. Zechariah 12:10,11,12
4. Zechariah 13:1
5. Joel 2:28,29,32
6. Zephaniah 3:9
7. Zechariah 14:3

8. Joel 3:2-16
9. Revelation 19:7
10. Revelation 19:8,9
11. Romans 8:17
12. I Thessalonians 4:17
13. II Timothy 2:12; Revelation 5:10
14. Revelation 19:14
15. II Thessalonians 1:7-9
16. Matthew 24:29,30
17. Zechariah 14:4
18. Revelation 19:17,18
19. Revelation 19:19
20. Revelation 19:11-16
21. Revelation 14:19,20
22. Revelation 16:6
23. Revelation 11:7-10
24. Romans 6:23

CHAPTER 15

Thy Kingdom Shall Come

A world without war or violence or crime? An earth that has become one vast Garden of Eden, with no violence and nothing to hurt or destroy? Believe it or not, it will someday become a reality!

But even the destruction of the armies of the world, and the casting of the Beast and the False Prophet into the lake of fire will not change the world overnight into a veritable paradise of beauty and peace. First, judgment must come. There never can be true peace until righteousness has been established. And righteousness follows God's judgment upon sin. He is not the indulgent, permissive Big Daddy up there. God is holy and demands holiness. He never compromises with iniquity. He will forgive but He will never condone or ignore sin. It must be paid its wages—death. And these wages must be paid either through appropriating the atoning death of Christ in faith, or they must be paid in person.

So when the battle of Armageddon has come to its gory end, there will be a judgment. Christ will be the Judge. Those still alive after the carnage of the Great Tribulation and Armageddon will be brought before the King of kings and Lord of lords. Jesus Himself describes the scene for us.

"When the Son of man shall come in his glory, and all the holy angels with him, then shall he sit upon the throne of his glory: And before him shall be gathered all nations: and he shall separate them one from another, as a shepherd divideth his sheep from the goats: And he shall set the sheep on his right hand, but the goats on the left.

"Then shall the King say unto them on his right hand, Come, ye blessed of my Father, inherit the kingdom prepared for you from the foundation of the world: For I was an hungred, and ye gave me meat: I was thirsty, and ye gave me drink: I was a stranger, and ye took me in: Naked, and ye clothed me: I was sick, and ye visited me: I was in prison, and ye came unto me.

"Then shall the righteous answer him, saying, Lord, when saw we thee an hungred, and fed thee? or thirsty, and gave thee drink? When saw we thee a stranger, and took thee in? or naked, and clothed thee? Or when saw we thee sick, or in prison, and came unto thee?

"And the King shall answer and say unto them,

Verily I say unto you, Inasmuch as ye have done it unto one of the least of these my brethren, ye have done it unto me."[1]

At that moment, the purging process that began with the judgments of the Great Tribulation and reached their peak with the battle of Armageddon will be resumed.

"Then shall he say also unto them on the left hand, Depart from me, ye cursed, into everlasting fire, prepared for the devil and his angels: for I was an hungred, and ye gave me no meat: I was thirsty, and ye gave me no drink: I was a stranger, and ye took me not in: naked, and ye clothed me not: sick, and in prison, and ye visited me not.

"Then shall they also answer him, saying, Lord, when saw we thee an hungred, or athirst, or a stranger, or naked, or sick, or in prison, and did not minister unto thee?

"Then shall he answer them, saying, Verily I say unto you, Inasmuch as ye did it not to one of the least of these, ye did it not to me.

"And these shall go away into everlasting punishment: but the righteous into life eternal."[2]

To whom was Jesus referring by His use of the term, "my brethren"?[3] Mark throws some light on this question.

"And then shall he send his angels, and shall gather together his elect from the four winds, from the uttermost part of the earth to the uttermost part of heaven."[4]

This interesting passage introduces us to the subjects of several prophecies.

1. *Those who will be slain by the Beast* because

they will not receive his blasphemous "Mark of the Beast" upon their forehead or their right hand, and will not worship his image. These are usually referred to as "The Tribulation Saints."[5]

John tells us that the souls of these martyrs shall cry out during the Great Tribulation for vengeance.[6]

2. *The Sealed Remnant of Israel*—the 144,000 who will be protected from the plagues of the Great Tribulation and the wrath of the Beast.[7]

Later in his vision, John sees this sealed remnant enjoying a position of special honor with Christ in His kingdom.[8]

3. *The Converts of the Two Witnesses and the Angel of Evangelism.* Since the Word of God cannot return void, it is not likely that the faithful ministry of the Two Witnesses would bear no fruit.[9] God always honors His Word. John says that there will be "saints" on earth during the Great Tribulation.[10]

After the murder of the Two Witnesses, God will not permit the earth to be without a messenger of the Gospel. John recorded, "And I saw another angel fly in the midst of heaven, having the everlasting gospel to preach unto them that dwell on the earth, and to every nation, and kindred, and tongue, and people, saying with a loud voice, Fear God, and give glory to him; for the hour of his judgment is come: and worship him that made heaven, and earth, and the sea, and the fountains of waters."[11]

Any one or all three of these groups could be those to whom Jesus referred as His "brethren."

During the reign of the Beast there will be those who, perhaps at the risk of their own lives, shelter and help those who are being hounded by the secret agents of the Beast. It has always been so. There are thousands of Jews now living in Israel who escaped to England or who were safely concealed from the human bloodhounds of Hitler by God-fearing Germans. Even the Antichrist will not enjoy one hundred percent success in his attempt to exterminate true godliness and righteousness. Some will escape, and there will be many who will help them to escape the wrath of the Beast.

There will be others who, for personal gain or from fear of detection or out of political or religious allegiance to the Beast, will refuse to aid the refugees. They will even hand them over to torture and death.

This judgment of the nations may be viewed as a prelude to the judgment of the Great White Throne which will occur a thousand years later.

Apparently those who refused to aid Christ's brethren will immediately go into everlasting punishment—possibly with the Beast and the False Prophet in the lake of fire.

Then "the Lord shall be king over all the earth: in that day shall there be one Lord, and his name one. . . . And it shall come to pass, that every one that is left of all the nations which came against Jerusalem shall even go up from year to year to worship the King, the Lord of hosts, and to keep the feast of tabernacles."[12]

In establishing His kingdom, the Lord Jesus Christ shall apply the rod of discipline to all the nations of the earth. Any act of disobedience will be immediately punished. Allegiance to the King of kings and Lord of lords will be obligatory.[13] All evil and unrighteousness will be uprooted. There will be universal justice for all men and by all men. Then, and then only, will this old earth be ready for the inauguration of that golden age, the Millennial reign of Christ.

Footnotes

1. Matthew 25:31-40
2. Matthew 25:41-46
3. Matthew 25:40
4. Mark 13:27
5. Revelation 13:15-17
6. Revelation 6:9-11
7. Revelation 7:1-8
8. Revelation 14:1-5
9. Revelation 11:3-7
10. Revelation 13:7
11. Revelation 14:6,7
12. Zechariah 14:9,16
13. Zechariah 14:18,19

CHAPTER 16

The Golden Age

Jesus' disciples came to Him requesting, "Lord, please teach us how to pray. John Baptist has taught his disciples and we also would like to learn to pray like you do."

And so, for the first time in human history, there came from the lips of men in prayer the words, "Our Father, which art in heaven."

The Jews had, of course, engaged in prayer. David had been a man of prayer. So had Abraham and Moses. In fact, prayer was a major part of the worship and the national life of the people of Israel. But never had they dared to call God their Father.

Enoch walked with God. Abraham became a friend of God. Moses talked face to face with God as a man speaks to his friend. David was a man after God's own heart. But not even these men ever thought of coming before God and saying, "Our Father."

Jesus continued the lesson on prayer. "Our Father, which art in heaven, Hallowed be thy name. Thy kingdom come. Thy will be done on earth as it is in heaven."

Ever since that first lesson, that same petition has ascended to the ears of God in ornate sanctuaries and by trundle beds. Men have preached about it, prayed for it and died waiting for the Kingdom of God to come. Misguided souls have talked about bringing in the kingdom through the expansion of the Church and through their own efforts at reform.

But the Kingdom of God cannot come until the will of God is done on earth as it is in heaven. The way the world is going today, it seems impossible that this could ever happen. But it will! The fulfillment of biblical prophecy will make it possible. And what will this world be like when that kingdom does come? The prophets describe it in glowing terms.

The Adamic curse will be lifted from nature.

"The wolf also shall dwell with the lamb, and the leopard shall lie down with the kid; and the calf and the young lion and the fatling together; and a little child shall lead them. And the cow and the bear shall feed; their young ones shall lie down together: and the lion shall eat straw like the ox. And the sucking child shall play on the hole of the asp, and the weaned child shall put his hand on the cockatrice's den [a creature so deadly that it was believed its glance was fatal]."[1]

The prophet Isaiah adds another touch of color to the rosy picture, "The wolf and the lamb shall feed together, and the lion shall eat straw like the bullock: and dust shall be the serpent's meat. They shall not hurt nor destroy in all my holy mountain, saith the Lord."[2]

Writing on the same subject, the apostle Paul commented, ". . . the creature [creation] itself also shall be delivered from the bondage of corruption into the glorious liberty of the children of God. For we know that the whole creation groaneth and travaileth in pain together until now . . . waiting for . . . the redemption . . ."[3]

There will be universal peace.

Christ shall "judge among the nations, and shall rebuke many people: and they shall beat their swords into plowshares, and their spears into pruninghooks: nation shall not lift up sword against nation, neither shall they learn war any more . . .[4] They shall not hurt nor destroy in all my holy mountain: for the earth shall be full of the knowledge of the Lord, as the waters cover the sea."[5]

Even the United Arab Republic will be at peace with Israel! Five major cities of Egypt will adopt Hebrew as their official language![6] An altar dedicated to the Lord God will be erected in the middle area of Egypt and shrines to Him shall be placed on her borders. The Word of God shall be taught in her schools and the Egyptians shall know the Lord Jesus Christ and offer oblations to Him.[7]

West Point and other military and naval academies will be closed. No young men will be conscripted for military duty. No warships will ply the oceans and no air force jets will leave their fleecy vapor trails in the sky. Nowhere in the world will a man in a military uniform be seen on the streets.

For the first time since the murder of Abel will this war-weary old earth know what universal peace is like. Imagine, if you can, an earth without war widows and prisoners of war! What a day that will be!

There will be unprecedented prosperity.

Isaiah tells us, "They shall feed in the ways, and their pastures shall be in all high places. They shall not hunger nor thirst; neither shall the heat nor sun smite them: for he that hath mercy on them shall lead them, even by the springs of water shall he guide them."[8]

Joel joins the joyous refrain, "And it shall come to pass in that day, that the mountains shall drop down new wine, and the hills shall flow with milk, and all the rivers of Judah shall flow with waters, and a fountain shall come forth of the house of the Lord, and shall water the valley of Shittim."[9]

"Be glad then, ye children of Zion, and rejoice in the Lord your God: for he hath given you the former rain moderately, and he will cause to come down for you the rain, the former rain, and the latter rain in the first month. And the floors shall be full of wheat, and the fats shall overflow with wine and oil. And I will restore to you the years that the locust hath eaten, the cankerworm, and the caterpiller, and the palmerworm, my great army which I sent among you. And ye shall eat in plenty, and be satisfied, and praise the name of the Lord your God, that he hath dealt wondrously with you: and my people shall never be ashamed."[10]

One explanation for the unprecedented prosperity that Israel will enjoy during the Golden Age is revealed to us by the prophet Ezekiel. He tells us that from under the threshold of the Temple in Jerusalem there will flow a stream of healing water. This stream will increase in volume as it flows eastward until it becomes a river.[11] Due to the massive earthquake at the second coming of Christ, the topography of the area will be completely changed. The Dead Sea will be raised from a level below the sea to an elevation above sea level. The healing river from Jerusalem will flow into it, and "the waters shall be healed. And it shall come to pass, that everything that liveth, which moveth, whithersoever the rivers shall come, shall live: and there shall be a very great multitude of fish, because these waters shall come thither: for they shall be healed; and everything shall live whither the river cometh."[12]

Imagine fishing in the Dead Sea! And that is not all. "Behold, at the bank of the river were very many trees on the one side and on the other . . . and by the river upon the bank thereof, on this side and on that side, shall grow all trees for meat [food], whose leaf shall not fade, neither shall the fruit thereof be consumed [exhausted]: it shall bring forth new fruit according to his months, because their waters they issued out of the sanctuary: and the fruit thereof shall be for meat, and the leaf thereof for medicine."[13]

There will be pleasant climatic conditions.

Some Bible students believe that prior to the great flood there was a heavy canopy of vapor high in the atmosphere, filtering the sunlight and protecting the earth from the dangerous cosmic and ultra violet rays. They base this opinion upon a statement found in the Genesis account of the creation, "And God made the firmament, and divided the waters which were under the firmament from *the waters which were above the firmament* . . ."[14] Those holding this viewpoint further believe that the collapse of this vapor canopy was one of the major causes of the great flood, quoting, ". . . the windows of heaven were opened."[15]

This theory goes one step further. It claims that during the Millennium, this vapor canopy will be restored. This would explain some of the statements made by the prophets regarding climatic and atmospheric conditions during the Golden Age. Let's look at some of these prophetic statements.

"And the Lord will create upon every dwelling place of mount Zion, and upon her assemblies, a cloud and smoke by day, and the shining of a flaming fire by night: for upon all the glory shall be a defense. And there shall be a tabernacle for a shadow in the daytime from the heat, and for a place of refuge, and for a covert from storm and from rain."[16]

"And it shall come to pass in that day, that the light shall not be clear, nor dark: but it shall be one day which shall be known to the Lord, not day, nor night: but it shall come to pass, that at evening time it shall be light."[17]

"Neither shall the heat nor sun smite them."[18] Just what this means we cannot be sure. For clearer details we will have to wait until we enter that Golden Age and see for ourselves how comfortable, how completely free from smog and sunburn the earth will be when it no longer suffers from the curse of sin.

There will be astonishing longevity.

When Christ reigns upon this earth and the yoke of depravity has been removed from man and nature, an amazing change will occur in man's physical condition. Isaiah provides us with this startling description of life during the Millennium, ". . . And there will no longer be heard in her [Jerusalem] the voice of weeping and the sound of crying. No longer will there be in it an infant who lives but a few days, or an old man who does not live out his days; for the youth will die at the age of one hundred and the one who does not reach the age of one hundred shall be thought accursed. And they shall build houses and inhabit them; they shall also plant vineyards and eat their fruit. They shall not build, and another inhabit, they shall not plant, and another eat; *for as the lifetime of a tree, so shall be the days of my people,* and my chosen ones shall wear out the work of their hands. They shall not labor in vain, or bear children for calamity; for they are the offspring of those blessed by the Lord."[19]

There will be divine comfort and security.

In that Golden Age, the redeemed will hear the voice of their beloved Lord, saying, "Fear thou not; for I am with thee: be not dismayed; for I am thy God: I will strengthen thee; yea, I will help thee; yea, I will uphold thee with the right hand of my righteousness."[20]

"Fear not: for I have redeemed thee, I have called thee by thy name; thou art mine. When thou passest through the waters, I will be with thee; and through the rivers, they shall not overflow thee: when thou walkest through the fire, thou shalt not be burned; neither shall the flame kindle upon thee."[21]

Perhaps, during that Golden Age the old and popular Christian song will become hit No. 1.

"And He walks with me, and He talks with me,
And He tells me I am His own;
And the joy we share as we tarry there,
None other has ever known."[22]

There will be worship in Spirit and in Truth.

This is one of the favorite themes of the Old Testament prophets.

Isaiah prophesied, "And it shall come to pass in the last days, that the mountain of the Lord's house shall be established in the top of the mountains, and shall be exalted above the hills; and all nations shall flow unto it.

"And many people shall go and say, Come ye, and let us go up to the mountain of the Lord, to the house of the God of Jacob; and he will teach us of his ways, and we will walk in his paths: for out of

Zion shall go forth the law, and the word of the Lord from Jerusalem."[23]

"And it shall come to pass, that every one that is left of all the nations which came against Jerusalem shall even go up from year to year to worship the King, the Lord of hosts, and to keep the feast of tabernacles . . . In that day shall there be upon the bells of the horses, HOLINESS UNTO THE LORD; and the pots in the Lord's house shall be like the bowls before the altar. Yea, every pot in Jerusalem and in Judah shall be holiness unto the Lord of hosts: and all they that sacrifice shall come and take of them, and seethe therein: and in that day there shall be no more the Canaanite [seller of merchandise] in the house of the Lord of hosts."[24]

In the Golden Age there will be no necessity for spending money to advertise the worship services. People will desire worship. They will hunger and thirst after righteousness. Zechariah tells us that people from one city will go to another community and say, "Let's get an excursion together for a prayer meeting in Jerusalem. We all want to go. How about going with us?"[25] This in itself will be heaven for many weary preachers.

From all over the world, from mighty nations there will be a constant stream of worshipers making their way to Jerusalem to worship the Lord Jesus Christ.[26] Every knee shall bow and every tongue shall confess that Jesus Christ is Lord, to the glory of God the Father.

This then will be THE GOLDEN AGE.

Footnotes

1. Isaiah 11:6-8
2. Isaiah 65:25
3. Romans 8:21-23
4. Isaiah 2:4
5. Isaiah 11:9
6. Isaiah 19:18
7. Isaiah 19:19-25
8. Isaiah 49:9-11
9. Joel 3:18
10. Joel 2:23-26
11. Ezekiel 47:1-5
12. Ezekiel 47:8,9
13. Ezekiel 47:7,12
14. Genesis 1:7
15. Genesis 7:11
16. Isaiah 4:5,6
17. Zechariah 14:6,7
18. Isaiah 49:10
19. Isaiah 65:19-23 (New American Standard Bible)
20. Isaiah 41:10
21. Isaiah 43:1,2
22. C. Austin Miles
23. Isaiah 2:2,3
24. Zechariah 14:16,20,21
25. Zechariah 8:20,21
26. Zechariah 8:22

CHAPTER 17

Goodbye, Old Earth

Would you like to have evidence of man's depravity? Is what David wrote of himself true of all men? "Behold, I was shapen in iniquity; and in sin did my mother conceive me."[1]

Is there reason to believe that Paul was exaggerating when he said, ". . . There is none righteous, no, not one: there is none that understandeth, there is none that seeketh after God. They are all gone out of the way, they are together become unprofitable; there is none that doeth good, no, not one . . . and the way of peace have they not known: there is no fear of God before their eyes"[2]?

Where can one find proof that Jeremiah's description of man's immoral nature is correct? Is the heart "deceitful above all things, and desperately wicked"[3]?

The evidence is to be found in biblical prophecy. For one thousand years Jesus Christ will be living and reigning on this earth. He will eliminate war, hunger, famine, strife, injustice, crime, even all elements of savagery from nature. The world will become one lovely Garden of Eden. His government will be benevolent and righteous. There will be nothing to hurt or destroy. Mankind will know a happiness it never dreamed possible.

During this time, Satan will be chained and imprisoned in the bottomless pit.[4] When the thousand years have expired, for a reason known only to God, Satan will be loosed and "shall go out to deceive the nations which are in the four quarters of the earth."[5] And then the incredible will happen!

After a thousand years with Christ, men—millions of them—will decide to go with Satan! Here is evidence of man's complete depravity. Satan will again succeed as he did in the original Garden of Eden! Once again men will choose to believe the lie and reject the truth.

The rebellion will originate in what is now known as Russia. Soon a vast army will be assembled and will march against Israel and the Christ of God. But there will be no battle. God the Father will now take matters into His own hands, and fire will fall from the skies and devour the rebels.[6]

Man's final effort to oppose God has failed. The end has come. Time is about to give way to eternity.

Not only man, but Satan also has reached the end of the road. What a thrill John must have felt as he penned the words, "And the devil that deceived them was cast into the lake of fire and brimstone, where the beast and the false prophet are, and shall be tormented day and night for ever and ever."[7]

And then what? The problem of Satan is settled for eternity. The Millennial reign of Christ on earth has come to a close. The last human resistance against the authority of God has been crushed with terrible judgment.

Peter picks up the story, ". . . the day of the Lord will come as a thief in the night; in the which the heavens shall pass away with a great noise, and the elements shall melt with fervent heat, the earth also and the works that are therein shall be burned up . . . all these things shall be dissolved . . . the heavens being on fire shall be dissolved, and the elements shall melt with fervent heat."[8] The apostle John adds, ". . . the earth and the heaven fled away; and there was found no place for them."[9] John's statement explains Peter's account of the end of the world.

Satan and man had destroyed God's earth until it was no longer fit for habitation.[10] Satan had invaded God's heaven as the accuser of God's children, and had so defiled it that a new heaven was necessary.[11]

To God, this was no problem. There would be a new heaven and a new earth. But first, the matter of sin had to be dealt with, once and forever. And John tells us how it will happen.

"And I saw a great white throne, and him that sat

on it, from whose face the earth and the heaven fled away . . . And I saw the dead, small and great, stand before God; and the books were opened: and another book was opened, which is the book of life: and the dead were judged out of those things which were written in the books, according to their works.

"And the sea gave up the dead which were in it; and death and hell delivered up the dead which were in them: and they were judged every man according to their works.

"And death and hell were cast into the lake of fire. This is the second death. And whosoever was not found written in the book of life was cast into the lake of fire."[12]

Who are these dead, "small and great," who will stand in judgment before the Great White Throne? Let's backtrack a bit and see who will *not* be involved in this final resurrection—the resurrection that will lead to "the second death."

At the Second Appearing of Christ, the dead in Christ will be resurrected to meet Christ in the air and be forever with Him. So this final resurrection could not include the Church.[13] Let's call the resurrection of the dead in Christ the first half of the first resurrection.

Then, at the second coming of Christ there will occur the second half of the first resurrection. John tells us about it.

"And I saw thrones, and they sat upon them, and judgment was given unto them: and I saw the souls of them that were beheaded for the witness of Jesus, and for the word of God, and which had not worshipped the beast, neither his image, neither had received his mark upon their foreheads, or in their hands; and they lived and reigned with Christ a thousand years.

"But the rest of the dead lived not again until the thousand years were finished. This is the first resurrection.

"Blessed and holy is he that hath part in the first resurrection: on such the second death hath no power, but they shall be priests of God and of Christ, and shall reign with him a thousand years."[14]

So the Tribulation Saints, those who were murdered by the Antichrist, will not be included in the final resurrection unto judgment. They, along with the Church, will have reigned with Christ on this earth for a thousand years before the time comes for the final resurrection.

How wonderful it is to know that our sins have been already judged at Calvary. We have died with Christ and in Christ. We who were dead in trespasses and sins have been quickened together with our wonderful Saviour. For us, there is no second death and no White Throne judgment. We can sing with the poet,

"Safe am I, Safe am I,
In the hollow of His hand."

Yes, heaven and earth shall pass away, "but he that doeth the will of God abideth forever."[15]

Footnotes

1. Psalm 51:5
2. Romans 3:10-12,17,18
3. Jeremiah 17:9
4. Revelation 20:1-3
5. Revelation 20:7,8
6. Revelation 20:8,9
7. Revelation 20:10
8. II Peter 3:10-12
9. Revelation 20:11
10. Revelation 11:18
11. Revelation 12:10
12. Revelation 20:11-15
13. I Thessalonians 4:16,17; I Corinthians 15:51-54
14. Revelation 20:4-6
15. I John 2:17

CHAPTER 18

The Second Death

Man can be born once and die twice; or he can be born twice and die once. In talking with Nicodemus, Jesus stressed the necessity of being born again "of the Spirit" into the family of God. Those who have been twice born will not suffer the second death. Those who never receive the Lord Jesus Christ have had only one birth experience—will die twice.

"It is appointed unto men once to die."[1] This is the fulfillment of the curse brought upon humanity through the sin of our first parents. There are, however, a few exceptions.

Enoch never died. He walked with God, and one day God said to him, "Enoch, instead of walking back to your home, suppose you come along with Me to My home." So God took him to heaven.[2]

Elijah never died. He rode a celestial whirlwind to heaven.[3]

Many Christians will never die. Those still alive at the Second Appearing of Christ will be changed into an immortal state. They will be caught up to meet the Lord in the air and will be with Him forever.[4]

John's prophecy makes it very clear that those who will suffer the second death are those whose names are not found written in the book of life when they stand before the Great White Throne of judgment.[5] Their position in life, their sincerity, their religious efforts—none of these will determine their final destiny.

Jesus said, "Not everyone that saith unto me, Lord, Lord, shall enter into the kingdom of heaven; but he that doeth the will of my Father which is in heaven.

"Many will say to me in that day, Lord, Lord, have we not prophesied in thy name? and in thy name have cast out devils? and in thy name done many wonderful works?

"And then will I profess unto them, I never knew you: depart from me, ye that work iniquity."[6]

The Great White Throne judgment will be the final one. The earth has suffered many judgments. There was the judgment of the curse upon Adam and Eve and their posterity. Then came the judgment of the flood in the days of Noah. Later, the

Jews suffered the judgment of the loss of their land and dispersion among the Gentiles. During the Great Tribulation the world will pass through three series of terrible judgments. The armies of the Antichrist will experience the judgment of Armageddon.

In addition to these, there are a number of major judgments to be found in history and prophecy.

The judgment of the believers' sins

Jesus said, ". . . He that heareth my word, and believeth on him that sent me, hath everlasting life, and shall not come into condemnation [judgment]; but is passed from death unto life."[7]

God made Christ to be sin for us, who knew no sin, so "that we might be made the righteousness of God in him."[8] "Once in the end of the world hath he appeared to put away sin by the sacrifice of himself . . . Christ was once offered to bear the sins of many . . ."[9]

The judgment of the believers' works

At the Second Appearing of the Lord Jesus Christ, all the members of His Church will stand before Him for an evaluation of their service, or lack of it.[10] Some will receive rich rewards. Some will find themselves empty-handed, all their works burned up because of wrong motives and they themselves saved as by fire.

The judgment of the nations

At the Second Coming of Christ, and after the battle of Armageddon, the people of the world will be brought before Christ and judged as to their treatment of His "brethren."[11]

The judgment of angels

It is probable that this judgment will occur when the Day of The Lord is ushered in and Satan is cast into the lake of fire. Jude tells us about it. "And the angels which kept not their first estate, but left their own habitation, he hath reserved in everlasting chains under darkness unto the judgment of the great day."[12] It is interesting that Christians will assist Christ in this judgment. "Know ye not that we shall judge angels?"[13] asked Paul.

The judgment of the Great White Throne

This final judgment will forever purge the universe of all sin. Never again will Satan be free to deceive and destroy. All creation will return to its original state of holiness and harmony with the will of God.

The subjects of this great judgment will be all the wicked dead from the dawn of human history until it merges with God's eternity. From the sea, from the graves of all the ages, the dead will be resurrected through the power of Jesus Christ. "For as in Adam all die, even so in Christ shall all be made alive."[14]

They will have come from all walks of life—the small and the great, young and old, rich and poor, male and female, but there will be one common denominator—all of them have never manifested repentance toward God and faith in the Lord Jesus Christ. Their names are not inscribed in the Lamb's book of life. And this is wickedness—the vilest sin of which man can be guilty.

The books of records will be opened and "the dead were judged out of those things which were written in the books, according to their works."[15] The last four words of this quotation, as well as other biblical references, would seem to indicate that there will be degrees of punishment in this final judgment. *All* will be eternally separated from the presence of God. But in a manner which we cannot understand at present there apparently will be degrees of punishment. ". . . He that knew not, and did commit things worthy of stripes, shall be beaten with few stripes. For unto whomsoever much is given, of him shall be much required: and to whom men have committed much, of him they will ask the more."[16]

The second death is everlasting separation from God, the Source of all light and hope and peace. It is the lake of fire. It is to be shut out from God and to be shut in with ". . . the fearful, and unbelieving, and the abominable, and murderers, and whoremongers, and sorcerers, and idolators, and all liars."[17]

There will be weeping and wailing and gnashing of teeth. There will be bitter, torturing memories of invitations rejected and prayers scorned. Apparently there will be the ability actually to see the glory and happiness of the blessed without an opportunity to share it.[18]

The Second Death will be night without the prospect of a dawn. It will be agony, physical and mental, with no hope for relief. It will be banishment with no possibility of reconciliation. It will be death that can never end in a resurrection. It will be an eternity of grief without one moment of peace. It will be everlasting, torturing memories without one night of sleep. It will be guilt without hope of pardon. It will be hell with no door to heaven.

THIS IS THE SECOND DEATH.

Footnotes

1. Hebrews 9:27
2. Genesis 5:22-24; Hebrews 11:5,6
3. II Kings 2:11
4. I Thessalonians 4:17
5. Revelation 20:15
6. Matthew 7:21-23
7. John 5:24
8. II Corinthians 5:21
9. Hebrews 9:26,28
10. Romans 14:10; II Corinthians 5:10
11. Matthew 25:31-46
12. Jude 6
13. I Corinthians 6:3
14. I Corinthians 15:22
15. Revelation 20:12
16. Luke 12:48
17. Revelation 21:8
18. Luke 16:23

CHAPTER 19

Good Morning, New Earth

There was a time in ages past when the Lord God looked upon His beautiful masterpiece of creation and said, "Behold, it [is] very good."[1] And it was, that is, until man permitted sin to enter and destroy its original purity.

But there will be a new creation—a new heaven and earth never to be marred by sin or defiled by Satan. And every thing in them will be good—very good—for all eternity. With his prophetic vision, John saw the glories of those endless ages—the new things which are being prepared for God's beloved children.

John saw the New Heaven.[2]

Apparently the new heaven did not make much

of an impression upon him. In fact, it seems that he did not give it even a second look. He tells us nothing whatever about it.

John saw the New Earth.[3]

It is not surprising that John's first impression of the new earth was that it had no sea. Exiled on the Isle of Patmos where night and day he heard the thundering of the surf, and surrounded by the waves which separated him from his beloved children in the faith, one can understand this first impression, "there was no more sea."

John observed a New Relationship on the new earth.

Whenever we think of God, we think of heaven. In that day, whenever we will think of God, we will think of earth. For God will leave His new heaven and come down and live with His people. "Behold, the tabernacle of God is with men, and he will dwell with them, and they shall be his people, and God himself shall be with them, and be their God."[4]

It will be a comforting new relationship. "God shall wipe away all tears from their eyes."[5] A little toddler falls and runs weeping into his mother's arms. She kisses the bruise, wipes away the tears from the chubby cheeks and says, "Now, everything is all right. Run along and play." So it will be on that new earth. God's children will run into His arms and He will wipe away all tears and kiss away forever all the hurts of this life, and there will be no more sorrow or crying.

It will be an endless relationship. "There shall be

no more death."[5] Neither sin or death will ever interrupt our fellowship with our Father. It will be a world without separations. Bereavement will not remain even as a memory. We will never lose any of our loved ones.

It will be a pain-free new relationship. "Neither shall there be any more pain"[5]—physical or emotional. Human relations usually involve painful situations to some degree. Human existence always includes its share of suffering. But not then! All "the former things are passed away."[5] Feelings will never get hurt and bodies will never ache. Malignancies and deadly viruses will never penetrate the new earth.

John saw the New City.[6]

And when he saw that New Jerusalem, his excitement was so great that his gaze never wandered. And what a sight it was! How would you like to have the responsibility of describing the colors of the rainbow . . . all the beauty of the flowers . . . everything beautiful and wonderful in this world to a person who had never left the darkness of an underground cavern? This was John's problem. How could he adequately describe a heavenly vision with an earthly language? Under the inspiration of the Holy Spirit, John did the best he could. But I have an idea that when we actually see it all, we will discover that its glory and beauty far surpass John's description.

About forty years before God provided this peek at glory, John was with his beloved Master and heard Him say, "Let not your heart be troubled: ye believe in God, believe also in me. In my Father's house are many mansions: if it were not so, I would have told you. I go to prepare a place for you. And if I go and prepare a place for you, I will come again, and receive you unto myself; that where I am, there ye may be also."[7]

John never forgot that prophetic promise. But little did he realize that he would see the prepared place before all the saints were gathered in.

Years ago I stood by what proved to be the deathbed of a saint of God. We thought he had gone to be with the Lord. There was no perceptible respiration. Suddenly his eyes opened wide, and in a clear strong voice, and with the light of heaven on his face, he said, "Oh, I had no idea it would be that wonderful, that glorious!" And then his eyes closed in death.

When John saw "that great city, the holy Jerusalem, descending out of heaven from God, having the glory of God,"[8] he noticed some interesting features. It shone like a crystal-clear jasper. It had a high wall with twelve gates, each gate having the name of one of the tribes of Israel. It had twelve foundation stones, each one inscribed with the name of one of the twelve apostles.

It was cubic in form, its height being equal to its length and breadth—fifteen hundred miles! Its wall measured two hundred and sixteen feet thick.

The wall was constructed of crystal-clear jasper and the city itself of gold. The foundation stones were inlaid with every kind of precious gem. Each gate was one gigantic pearl. The street of the city was made of gold, so pure it was transparent.

Then John noticed what the city did not have.

It had no temple.[9] It needed none. No indirect approach to God was necessary. God was there in the city—anywhere and everywhere.

It had no sun or moon.[10] Its luminary was a living Person—God Himself. God was its glory, and the Lamb was its lamp. The city itself served as the source of light for the new earth.[11]

Now, suppose we walk into the city with John and see what its interior looks like.

The throne of God is in it.[12] It is the center of the universe.

A river flows from under the throne and down through the center of the street. A street wide enough for a river to flow down its center? Of course. This is the *New* Jerusalem. That is not all. On both sides of the river there is an orchard of THE TREE OF LIFE! This is the tree that was in the Garden of Eden. And because it was there, God evicted Adam and Eve from the garden lest they eat of the fruit of the tree of life and live forever in their sinful state.[13] Now, God puts a sign in His orchard, "Help yourself."

And the fruit of the tree of life is not confined to one specie. Each month the tree bears a different kind of fruit. And even its leaves are useful. They are for the healing of the nations living outside the city on the new earth.[14]

And best of all the Lamb is there, and we shall see His face and He will give to us, as His bride, His own name. And with Him we shall reign forever and ever—everywhere, over all His universe![15]

"O that will be glory for me;
When by His grace I shall look on His face,
That will be glory, be glory for me."[16]

Yes, the believer will be home at last. And we shall discover that "eye hath not seen, nor ear heard, neither have entered into the heart of man, the things which God hath prepared for them that love him."[17]

Why not close this study with a message from our wonderful Lord!

"Behold, I come quickly; and my reward is with me, to give every man according as his work shall be . . . I Jesus have sent mine angel to testify unto you these things in the churches . . . He which testifieth these things saith, Surely I come quickly."[18]

Instead of saying, "Amen," let's join with John in saying, "Even so, come, Lord Jesus."[19]

Footnotes

1. Genesis 1:31
2. Revelation 21:1
3. Revelation 21:1
4. Revelation 21:3
5. Revelation 21:4
6. Revelation 21:9–22:5
7. John 14:1-3
8. Revelation 21:10,11
9. Revelation 21:22
10. Revelation 21:23
11. Revelation 21:24
12. Revelation 22:1
13. Genesis 3:22

14. Revelation 22:2
15. Revelation 22:3-5
16. Charles H. Gabriel
17. I Corinthians 2:9
18. Revelation 22:12,16,20
19. Revelation 22:20

Chronology of Prophecy

The Last Perilous Days 1972–

Decline in love and spiritual worship

Increase in apostasy and cultism

Knowledge and travel explosion

The Second Appearing of Christ

The resurrection of the dead in Christ

The changing of the living believers into an immortal state

Both are caught up together to meet the Lord in the air

The Judgment of the Christians at the Judgment Seat of Christ

Every man's work tried as by fire

Some shall receive a reward

Others see all their works burned

The Antichrist Appears and the Great Tribulation Begins

He restores prosperity and order

Establishes a ten-kingdom confederacy

The False Prophet Appears and Proclaims the Antichrist as God

He performs miracles

Erects a statue of the Antichrist in the Temple and causes it to live and speak

Performs miracles and lying wonders

The Two Witnesses Are Sent by God

They expose the false claims of the Antichrist

Perform miracles and bring judgments

Are murdered by the Antichrist and the world rejoices

After three and a half days they are raised to life and ascend to heaven

The Antichrist and His Armies Invade Jerusalem

The Jews Turn to God

The Second Coming of Christ

The Battle of Armageddon

The Judgment of the Nations

Satan Is Bound

The Kingdom of Christ Is Established on Earth

Satan Is Loosed and Again Deceives the Nations

Fire destroys the forces attacking Jerusalem

Heaven and Earth Pass Away

The Great Resurrection

The Judgment of the Great White Throne

New Heaven and New Earth with Its New Jerusalem